CAREGIVING

When Someone You Love Grows Old

CARE GIVING

When Someone You Love Grows Old

by John Gillies

Harold Shaw Publishers
Wheaton, Illinois

ISBN 0-87788-104-9

Cover photo © 1988, Robert McKendrick

Library of Congress Cataloging-in-Publication Data

Gillies, John, 1925-
    Caregiving : when someone you love grows old / John Gillies.
        p. cm.—(Heart and hand series)
    Rev. ed. of: A guide to caring for and coping with aging parents. 1981.
    Bibliography: p.
    Includes index.
    ISBN 0-87788-104-9 (pbk.)
    1. Parents, Aged—United States. 2. Parents, Aged—United States—Family relationships. 3. Adult children—United States. 4. Aged—Care—United States. I. Gillies, John, 1925- Guide to caring for and coping with aging parents. II. Title. III. Series.
HQ1063.6.G55 1988
646.7'8—dc19   87-33310
                                                        CIP

---

97   96   95   94   93   92   91   90   89   88
10   9   8   7   6   5   4   3   2   1

Contents

Preface

Today there is a new awareness of aging. Much is written about the subject. Even White House consultations have been held to establish new government agencies to deal with problems of the aging. Workshops and seminars are common. And all of this is good and long overdue, for we are living longer and growing older.

In 1900 only one North American out of 25 was over 65 years of age. Today it's closer to one out of eight. And this trend is worldwide. While the world's population is growing by an estimated 1.7 percent annually, the 65 + population grows by 2.4 percent.

Nine countries now have more than one million citizens age 80 or over: the United States, China, the Soviet Union,

India, Japan, West Germany, France, the United Kingdom, and Italy. Japan's life expectancy is the highest of any developed nation; it's 77 years. In the U.S., it's 74.6.

Every day approximately 5,000 North Americans turn 65 and about 3,600 older persons die. Thus, our older population is constantly growing and will continue to grow because of better medical care and improved nutritional habits.

So much for statistics. What about the human side?

Most of our older people are women. There are five times as many widows as widowers. And women have the highest poverty rate in our nation.

Because birthrates are down in most Western "developed" countries, there are fewer taxpayers to contribute to social security programs. The elderly face economic problems, as fixed incomes do not keep up with inflation, or savings evaporate through illness or other emergencies.

The nuclear family is disappearing—through divorce, mobility, or smaller living areas—and this affects the old as well as the young.

Nevertheless the image that most elderly persons are feeble and senile is wrong. Happily, most older people are able to manage on their own. Eighty out of 100 of them live independently; they are the *frisky* elderly. Fifteen of those 100 may still try to live independently, but require occasional help; these are the *failing* or *frail* elderly. Only five from this cluster of 100 receive some kind of custodial care, most likely in a nursing home; they are the *fragile* elderly.

This book is written for those persons who have a responsibility for those twenty percent of the elderly, the frail and the fragile.

You may be one of these caregivers. Some have named you the "sandwich generation." Just when your children are grown and you begin to contemplate future pleasure and leisure, some older person you love has an accident or becomes seriously ill, and once again you face responsibility for another human being. If that loved one is a parent, you may have become a parent to your parent.

If you are not yet a caregiver, you probably know someone who is. I've learned from my experience that each of us will be better caregivers if we prepare for the role. If we begin to do a few things for ourselves *now* that will help us to cope *then,* we may be able to delay entering that twenty percentile of "failing and fragile."

What You Can Expect from This Book

This is not a technical book on gerontology or a book on the rights of older persons. Others have written such books. It's not a book about what the church or community groups ought to be doing for their older members. I've done that in my companion book *A Guide to Compassionate Care of the Aging.*

So what is this book? Partly a record of our learned experiences—our initial confusion, subsequent convictions, stories of how we did it. But I hope it offers something else—practical advice to make your path in caring for your aging loved one a little easier. If at times it sounds as though we found *the* answer for a given situation or problem, then I have recounted the experience badly. My wife, Carolyn, and I were caregivers for eleven years. We learned as we lived out our caregiving, just as you will learn.

Paul Lewis Young, my father-in-law, went to Ecuador as a missionary in 1918; he was one of the five pioneers who began radio station HCJB in Quito. Twice-widowed, he commuted between his retirement home in Florida and Ecuador, and one day surprised us with his announcement that he planned to marry again. The day before his wedding, following the rehearsal, Paul had a massive stroke which paralyzed his right side and left him a hemiplegic and an "expressive aphasic." The frequent change in altitude from the Andes to sea level in Florida probably took its toll. Later we found his medication for high blood pressure, which he had forgotten to take with him, in the trunk of his car.

Paul lived for eight years—two months in a Minneapolis hospital, seven months in a Florida nursing home, and the remainder of his life with us in Texas, both in our home and in a long-term health facility.

My mother, Anna, also a missionary (to Lithuania), was a victim of Alzheimer's, although we did not know the term when our caregiving began. For eleven years we watched and helped Anna through independent living, residential care (known as "congregate living"), care in our home, and finally, nursing home care. She never became violent but her deterioration was steady, irreversible, and very sad. She did not recognize us during the last three years of her life. We mourned our loss, and hers, long before she died.

We cared for Paul and Anna concurrently. At the beginning, one of our three children, a teenage son, was still living at home. Thus, we know how it feels to be the "sandwich generation." Throughout this book I will refer to Paul and Anna. It could not be otherwise.

As Carolyn and I look back, we admit that it wasn't an easy road. There are things we know now that we wish we had known then, things that would have made the caring and coping easier. But we also want you to understand that it wasn't a constant trial. We found many friends who helped, and we certainly discovered that God's grace, especially in caregiving, is sufficient, wonderful, and joyful. As a result, we are now better able to face our own aging, without intimidation and certainly with less fear.

John Gillies

1
What's Your Perspective on Aging?

In order to be thoughtful and helpful caregivers, we need to take stock of this business of aging.

We begin to age as soon as we are born. Our hair falls out, eyesight and hearing fail, muscles shrink, joints twist, and skin wrinkles. The rate of change is affected by a variety of factors: where we live, what we eat, our heredity, and our work environment. Some people appear ancient at fifty-five. Others remain vivacious and sharp-witted at ninety-five. Many people now question whether anyone should be pressured to retire at age sixty-five. It depends on the individual.

There's a difference between *senescence* and *senility.* Senescence is growing old, maturing, aging. We can think of it as a kind of "ripening." Senility describes a feebleness of body and mind, a deterioration that is often irreversible. Too often we label people "senile" when they may be suffering from depression, nutritional deficiencies, tumors, infections, or overmedication and drug interactions. These kinds of conditions can be treated and helped.

Robert Browning wrote, "Grow old along with me, the best is yet to be." For many fortunate "oldsters," Browning's promise has proved true—there are still "golden years" at the end of life.

Life in late years can be happy and productive. We have been unduly conditioned by advertising and the media that "young is beautiful." We spend eight times as much on cosmetics as we do on public care for the aging. Ponce de Leon sought his "fountain of youth" long ago, and we refuse to give up the search.

Myths about Old Age

Bert Kruger Smith, author of *Aging in America,* admonishes us to discard four myths regarding older Americans.

First, she says, it is a myth that *older people cannot learn:* "You can't teach an old dog new tricks." But you can. Meaningful opportunities and stimuli for older citizens have demonstrated their potential for learning.

A second myth is that *sexual interest and activity is limited to the young.* God's gift of sexuality is not limited.

2

Such biblical characters as Abraham, Boaz, and David are good examples.

To be sure, some live-in arrangements among older people are due more to economics than affection. While it was never true that two can live as cheaply as one, two unmarried people can collect larger Social Security checks if they remain "single" and pool their benefits.

Paul Young, my father-in-law, was about to be married for the third time (he was widowed twice) when he had his stroke. I am sure that his intentions, even at age eighty-three, were not merely platonic or spiritual. He wanted a companion and a wife.

Many newer nursing home facilities encourage husbands and wives to share rooms. Many homes also provide visiting rooms, away from the public lounges, for those residents who want a more private setting for conversation and, I fully believe, for romance.

Smith points to a third myth—*older people do not want to work*. Many physically able persons prefer to work beyond mandatory retirement age, not so much because of the income (important as that is in times of inflation) but because they want to feel needed and useful. Paul commuted between Florida and Ecuador well into his eighties. Until Anna broke a hip and could no longer walk and explore, she remained physically active even when her mind had ceased to function. Many groups are discovering the valuable contributions of time and skills older volunteer workers can provide.

The fourth myth Mrs. Smith cites is that *older people*

like to be helpless. It is often hard for me to restrain myself from giving help, especially when a loved one is handicapped and a clear danger exists. Nevertheless, Smith reminds us that most older people, even those who are handicapped, prize whatever degree of independence is still available to them.

Not every older person is forgetful. Some do like to reminisce and tend to remember what was exciting and adventuresome in their youth and forget what happened yesterday. But many older people can still recite the Apostles' Creed and portions of Scripture or sing hymns from memory.

Older people are not necessarily happiest when they are with other older people. Many prefer to remain within familiar neighborhoods and shopping facilities, where a mix of ages exists. Churches and other groups can provide opportunities for bridging generation gaps and creating new friendships. Sometimes an older person requires the sense of comfort and security of being in the company of peers, but very few want this to be their *only* company.

Older people do not necessarily have all their personal and spiritual accounts settled. Some elderly people still harbor grudges and waste away with bitterness. Like the rest of us, they need to find forgiveness from friends, family, and God. They may even need to forgive themselves.

Are We Inventing New Myths?
As we demythologize aging, however, let's not invent new myths.

One of these is the blind belief that the notion of "the best is yet to be" applies to everyone past sixty-five. A vast institutional population would not agree—nor would their families.

The American Association of Retired Persons (AARP), of which I am a member, has an advertising policy for its magazine that seems to close its eyes to reality. Advertising of wheelchairs and incontinence products is not accepted, but advertising of lush travel sites and retirement spas is extensive in every issue. Even though the majority of oldsters can and do enjoy life, that good life is not enjoyed by every older person.

Old isn't always beautiful. An old building may be a beautifully preserved historical landmark—or a tenement. A chair may be a highly polished and elegant antique—or a broken piece of junk. Beauty is always in the eye of the beholder, and remembering what *was* distorts what *is*. More than a million older people in the United States live in environments and situations devoid of hope, and for them old is not beautiful.

So the quest for perpetual youth continues.

There are some amazing older people! I was thrilled with Arthur Rubinsteins's superb concert, given on his ninetieth birthday. I was amazed and pleased to hear Averell Harriman—at age eighty-seven—discuss international affairs with great lucidity. They and other fortunate ones like them are examples of perseverance and strength, but they are *not* examples of perpetual youth.

Perhaps we should be more cautious in suggesting that everyone be allowed to work or drive as long as he wishes or appears to be able, that little risk exists, that the latter years are *always* "golden years" of creativity and wisdom. I wish those myths *were* fact.

In a workshop recently I used the word *senility* and was gently clobbered by a couple of people who said I should talk about "progressive deterioration" or "progressive dementia" instead. Apparently this is a way to attack "ageism" in our culture, just as others attack "sexism" in our language.

Bert Kruger Smith and others help us to identify and discard the myths that distort our perception of older people. We are not ageless, and one of the risks of living is that some of us age faster than others.

We do die daily, but we don't want to be reminded that there will be an end to life. Perhaps this is why strong, able older people don't really enjoy visiting deteriorating, handicapped older people.

Somehow we must come to terms with our own deterioration. We must find and maintain a balanced perspective on aging if we are to help those who struggle for meaning, worth, and reality.

I'm blessed with many older friends—people in their seventies, eighties, and nineties—friends who enjoy thinking and probing life and current events.

But it's much different with frail and fragile older people who are failing in mobility, in sight, in hearing, and most sadly, in mind. These are the kinds of older people this book is about.

Signs of Sensory Loss

Hearing loss affects nearly a third of the elder population. It affects more men than women. It may cause irrational thinking because of missing verbal information or instruction. Results are often social isolation, depression, suspicion, and sometimes, ridicule.

If hearing loss is confirmed by an audiological exam, hearing may be improved through medical treatment or hearing aids. You can communicate more effectively with a person with a hearing loss if you face the person, speak slowly and distinctly (you don't have to shout), use body language including touch, and avoid the confusion of several persons trying to speak at the same time, as in a group conversation.

Vision. One in five older persons has impaired vision. Women are affected more than men. Visual impairment limits mobility and affects orientation. Eye exams may show the need for surgery or for new corrective lenses. Cataract surgery may be required. Take advantage of large print books, hand magnifiers, and clocks and calendars with large numbers.

Taste. This sensory loss is often overlooked and is frequently the reason for nursing home residents' complaints about the quality of food. After age 50, our ability to taste *quality* (sweet, sour, salty, bitter) declines. After age 60, most persons lose half of their taste buds. The salty-sweet taste buds at the front of the tongue atrophy first. Very little can be done to correct this condition, but it helps to understand what is happening. Because a person does not taste "saltiness" they may use too much salt, and this should be monitored. Don't assume that all elderly people are content with bland diets. Certain safe condiments may make foods more palatable and are an acceptable way to get elderly persons to eat the foods they need.

Balance. As persons grow older they may feel less secure in "spatial orientation." They may complain of dizziness and buzzing in their ears. Loss of balance results in falls. Rearrange furniture in rooms so there is something to hold onto or install handrails or grab bars. In a nursing home environment there should be adequate benches or places to sit and rest.

Touch. This sense stays with us the longest. There may be some decline in feeling, but the need for the intimacy of touch remains strong. Provide opportunities for touch: familiar objects, a prized shawl or sweater, or a pet. Be generous with handshakes and embraces.

Keep in mind that grief occurs whenever there is a severe loss. This is most obvious with the death of a mate. But older persons grieve when they lose hearing or sight—or sense that they are having memory loss. Such grief can cause depression. You will be a better caregiver as you recognize the symptoms and the results—and as you help your loved one through these various dark valleys of deterioration.

2
Alternatives You Should Consider

Once upon a time, families did not move much. Wage-earners did not change jobs every two to four years. American families lived in rural areas or small towns. Houses were big, and families were large. Mothers stayed at home to care for the family while fathers worked. It was expected that father and mother, and grandfather and grandmother, would end their years in their own homes, probably only a few doors or blocks from the homes of their children (if not actually in their children's homes).

Before the era of technological inventions that made home care and cooking easier, faster, and more efficient, there were enough essential chores for every member of the family. The old folks were needed at home.

We see some of this older tradition still in the Amish communities. But for most of us, this era has passed. Our homes and our families are smaller. It is no longer practical to take aging parents with us when we move, even if they wanted to come, and even if we had the room.

The ideal situation for our parents is still the one where they can manage their lives without interference and intervention—a situation that enables them to live, shop, garden, socialize, and worship where and as they wish. There are ways we may be helpful in facilitating such independent living for them.

When totally independent living is no longer possible, several alternatives exist. We will look at some of these in greater detail later. In summarizing the alternatives here I want to emphasize that the nursing home is by no means the *only* alternative to independent living.

Independent Living

Your aging loved ones may have a home or an apartment in which they may continue to live. If they own their own property and it isn't too large for them to handle, they should be encouraged to hold on to such accommodations. They'll be happier and their living costs will be lower.

If a loved one has recently suffered an accident or some handicapping illness, it may be necessary to do some remodeling, particularly in kitchens and bathrooms. More specifics will be detailed in Chapter 3.

Find ways to check on independent loved ones and their

situation without destroying their independence. You need to be sure of their capabilities. Regular visits will allow you to see if things are under control. Perhaps you could take responsibility for heavier chores—putting up storm windows, weatherstripping, or making certain repairs. If you live some distance away, arrange for a neighbor or a nearby friend to check on them by telephone and in person; it's helpful to have a third person's reaction and evaluation.

Keep in frequent telephone contact. Install a telephone if your loved ones don't have one or no longer feel they need one. Be sure it's conveniently placed—or arrange for an additional extension at their bedside. Consider a telephone with memory; program emergency numbers, including your own. The TV commercials are true—it *is* possible to reach out and touch, to show love and concern by the warmth of your voice. You can discern much of the emotional and physical well-being of loved ones by hearing them speak—or not speak.

A telephone is essential in emergencies. Affix a list of emergency numbers to each telephone in your loved ones' home. Include the local doctor's number and your own telephone number (identify it so a stranger would know whom to call first).

Find out if there is a telephone reassurance program in the city where your loved ones live. Such programs are sponsored by civic groups or churches and provide older people with a number they can call anytime to reach someone who will listen and help.

Retirement Centers

Retirement communities are becoming increasingly available and popular. They range from clusters of individual units to high-rise apartment-type dwellings. "The Governor's" and "The Whitestone," where Anna lived, were remodeled university residences that provided "congregate" or "sheltered" living.

Living space will always be reduced in such facilities, and parents must decide which personal items they will retain. A few keepsakes and favorite pieces of furniture help to bridge the change from a former home to a new residence, which in time ought to become *home*.

Some retirement centers provide a dining room where meals may be eaten in a cafeteria or restaurant setting. Sometimes only noon and evening meals are served, allowing the resident to prepare his or her own breakfast. Often a choice is available—he may eat with others in a dining room or prepare meals in his own room or apartment.

Some centers are built next to convalescent facilities, but retirement communities are not nursing homes. They provide no medical assistance and are prohibited by law from doing so. Residents must usually be ambulatory and be able to care for themselves. A few centers provide what is called a "life care" guarantee—which includes future nursing care whenever needed—but such arrangements are costly.

Retirement centers have the advantages of pleasant surroundings without the need to keep up a yard. Security is provided around the clock. There is value in sharing a common, caring life within a community that offers stimulating activities and involvement for active older citizens.

Since costs and plans vary, retirement residences should be investigated carefully, perhaps with legal advice. If federal funding helped build such a retirement facility, there is usually no down-payment required. Monthly "rents" are adjusted to one's income. Such housing may have been built by a municipality or a nonprofit organization or church.

Privately financed facilities always require some kind of down-payment. Such entrance fees can be substantial, and high monthly "maintenance" assessments may also be required. Down-payments may be nonrefundable or in the form of required purchase of bonds or annuities. Read the prospectus and contract carefully before signing it. Do the proceeds of the entrance fee revert to the sponsoring organization upon the resident's death, or do they become part of the resident's estate? What are the rights of the surviving spouse?

Ask whether pets and gardens are allowed. These are important to many retirees. What restrictions are there, if any, for "normal" living?

Don't make a decision merely on the basis of a printed brochure or prospectus, a telephone conversation, or even someone's recommendation. Visit the facility. Observe and evaluate it for yourself, with your parent if possible. Take your time when you visit. If it is permitted, have a meal there. Observe the ongoing activities and facilities for hobbies. How close are shopping centers and churches? Is the facility in the country or in the city? Is public transportation available—or accessible? If possible, chat with residents and get their reactions. A future home is involved, so make this a joint decision.

Day Activities Centers

Many groups now sponsor supervised day-care or day activities centers for older persons. These are held in churches, in storefront facilities, or in new specially designed neighborhood centers. Activities include games, crafts, "reality therapy" (I'll explain this term later), exercise, field trips, shopping sprees, special programs of slides and music, conversation, and a well-balanced hot noon meal (sometimes provided through a delivered-meal or "meals-on-wheels" program). Transportation is sometimes provided by the center. Participants must usually be ambulatory, be able to help and serve themselves, and manage restroom needs on their own.

In some areas where nursing home occupancy is down, nursing homes are cooperating with state social service agencies to develop day-care activities centers within nursing home facilities. Since some nursing or paramedical staff is available, wider participation—including that of handicapped persons—is possible.

The purpose of a day activity center is to provide a safe, secure, and exciting place for an older person to spend the day, whether he or she lives independently or in the home of a friend or relative.

Foster Care or Group Care

Because welfare agencies are seeking alternatives to expensive nursing home care, increasing attention is being given to new models of group (or "sheltered") living that might provide supportive and safe care for the aging.

Just as some families take in children with special needs, foster homes for adults with special needs are also being sought. A couple or family who owns a large home might be able to provide shelter and food for three or four adults. One or both "foster helpers" may be eligible to receive compensation for their labor as well as for providing room and board. Necessary nursing care might be provided through a public health service or some other approved provider of home medical care.

A foster home may be preferable for those who require some medical and custodial care but not the twenty-four-hour skilled care that nursing homes are designed to provide—and for which charges must be higher. In many cases, a good foster home provides a happier and less structured environment than a nursing home or even a relative's home. Those in the group help one another.

Sometimes grouping or association is spontaneous. Three to five individuals might discover a compatibility and decide to rent a house or apartment together, sharing expenses and responsibilities. Women, particularly widows with limited resources, frequently combine funds and interests in some common arrangement. Today this is called "congregate living."

There is nothing new about sharing a large house or

apartment with others; boardinghouses and tourist homes were precursors of this idea. What *is* new is the possibility of securing reimbursement from state agencies for "chore care" or "homemaker" services. Social service agencies are seeking innovative ways to extend the value of inflated dollars, while keeping persons not requiring skilled care out of nursing homes.

Most welfare agencies have an administrative unit dealing with the "aged, blind, and disabled" (sometimes called ABD programs) that can provide you with information about day activities centers and group-care facilities in your area.

Nursing Homes

Chapter 4 will discuss nursing homes in greater detail— particularly the criteria for choosing one. For now, let's just say that there *is* a place for nursing homes in the spectrum of care for the aging. These homes provide necessary services.

A nursing home is not a way station on the road to the cemetery. Too many elderly people (and their children) have this image of nursing homes and balk at even considering them.

Many states require nursing homes to devise a release plan (which may include a rehabilitation or resident care program) for every resident upon admission. It is a worthy goal. Many older patients who merely require convalescence should not pay the high cost of hospital care. Use of hospital beds should be limited to emergencies, serious illnesses requiring specialized equipment and facilities, or intensive postoperative care. Nursing homes can and do provide intermediate and short-term care; they used to be called "convalescent homes."

There may be times when an older person receiving care in your home should become a temporary resident in a nursing home. Your family may face an emergency that requires this, or you may need a vacation to get away from the stress of providing constant health care.

Nursing homes also provide long-term care. A person who requires around-the-clock medication, who needs an ongoing therapy program, or who is incontinent or generally disoriented may require the special, skilled care that only a good nursing home can provide. If it is advised by your physician, explore the possibilities of nursing homes without feeling guilty or morbid.

Hospices

The dictionary defines *hospice* as "a place of shelter for travelers." The Latin word means "hospitality." In medieval times such way stations were usually maintained by monastic orders.

When Dr. Cicely Saunders opened St. Christopher's Hospice in London, England in 1967, a new approach to care for the terminally ill was established. Now there are several hundred hospices in the United States, the United Kingdom, and Europe. Their growth is limited by finances, the need for government approval and licensing, and massive opposition by segments of the commercial nursing home industry.

Hospices provide support services to families who keep terminally ill loved ones at home. They also provide institutional care facilities—small, pleasant, hospital-type structures, usually with less than fifty beds. Hospices care for those who have been diagnosed as having a terminal disease (usually cancer) for which the life expectancy is six months or less.

Hospices treat symptoms, not diseases. Medication is given for pain. Care is provided by physicians, nurses, social workers, pastors or pastoral counselors, psychiatrists, therapists, pharmacologists, family members, and volunteers in a holistic manner. Support is given not only to the patient, but also to the patient's family.

A few physicians have felt called to this new kind of ministry—*new* because in so many ways the hospice approach goes against a background and an education of physicians that has as its only objective helping people to get well.

The hospice movement helps patients and families to face death with dignity and security, surrounding them with loving care and concern.

Sandol Stoddard, in her book *The Hospice Movement* (Briarcliff Manor, NY: Stein and Day, 1977) provides this description:

People in hospices are not attached to machines, nor are they manipulated by drips or tubes, or by the administration of drugs that cloud the mind without relieving pain. Instead, they are given comfort by methods sometimes rather sophisticated but often amazingly simple and obvious, and they are helped to live fully in an atmosphere of loving kindness and grace until the time has come for them to die a natural death. It is a basic difference in attitude about the meaning and value of human life, and about the significance of death itself which we see at work in the place called *hospice*.

This newest alternative in caring for loved ones who are dying is one many families may want to consider. The atmosphere in hospices is one of joy and celebration and hope—surely an atmosphere with which people of faith can identify.

3
A Special Look at Home Care

Health care for your loved one—whether in your own home or in another—requires planning, patience, and modification of both your home and your life-style. Sometimes the planning enters into your selection of a new home. When Carolyn and I returned to live in Austin, we had already decided that we would provide a place in our home for Anna.

"Independent" Living
Although Anna was showing increasing signs of disorientation, she was able to walk and to care for most of her needs. We felt she needed some independence but that

she also needed family close by. In our house-hunting Carolyn and I looked at single-family dwellings that offered a "mother-in-law" design—a bedroom with bath at the end of the house opposite from where the rest of the family would be living.

What we found were homes either prohibitive in cost or impractical in design. Most "mother-in-law" arrangements were built adjacent to the kitchen or dining/living area. We felt that such proximity would inhibit what little entertaining we did, as well as the more boisterous habits of our teenage son.

We finally purchased a four-bedroom home, with all four bedrooms located in the same general area. We assigned the master bedroom to Anna because it had its own bath and was large, allowing Anna plenty of room to spread out her things and to work on projects.

Since Anna preferred to get up later than the rest of the family, we purchased a small three cubic-foot refrigerator and stocked it with milk, juices, and fruit so she could make her own breakfast. We bought a hot pot for her to boil water or heat soup when she wanted a snack. We wanted her to feel some independence, but we also encouraged and expected her to eat her other two meals with the rest of the family.

It wasn't a bad arrangement. The criteria we established are valid for families who can afford a house with this much room, allowing for some independent living without exclusion from the family. The trick is to balance independence with realistic dependence.

Then Anna began to wander off and get lost. She rarely ate breakfast and became careless about her personal hygiene. She was confused about her volunteer work with children at the day-care center. It was evident that she was no longer able to cope with this level of independent living. The next stage was the retirement center.

Modify or Remodel?

We learned a great deal from having Anna in our home, and we made new plans before Paul arrived.

First Carolyn and I moved into the master bedroom. Paul would use the smaller bedroom we had used. During his seven months in a Florida nursing home, Paul had lived in a semi-private room. Now he would have a room to himself again. Since he was a hemiplegic (paralyzed on his right side) and could walk only with assistance, we guessed he would have difficulty maneuvering his wheelchair through our relatively narrow hallway and over our wall-to-wall shag carpet. We had to plan some modification that would not totally alter our house nor upset the family and its routine.

Andy, our youngest son, was completing his senior year of high school. For several months, he and Paul would have to share the same bathroom. That would require planning and patience on Andy's part.

My first step was to build ramps at the front entrance and the patio entrance. They had to be sturdy but not heavy and easily movable for sweeping and cleanup underneath. This problem was solved rather easily.

But the carpet gave us more trouble. We tried a long plastic runner in the hallway, but soon gave up on that idea. The plastic never stayed flat, and we didn't like the odor. We finally decided that since we were not about to rip out our carpet, Paul would simply have to get used to the shag. We would push his wheelchair and assist him with his walker as he made his way to his favorite chairs. He was able to maneuver his wheelchair alone outdoors on the concrete patio.

If you live in a two-story house, you might want to set aside a room at ground level for your loved one's use. If this isn't practical, and if your loved one cannot negotiate stairs, consider the lease or purchase of a stair elevator. They can be installed in several hours, with no structural change or additional wiring required in your house.

You also might want to make some provision for easier communication within the house. Intercom units can be purchased in radio supply stores.

We decided we didn't need this much modern technology for our particular needs. I purchased an ordinary bicycle bell and mounted it on Paul's wheelchair; he rang it when he needed our attention. A bicycle squeeze-type horn beside his bed could be used in an emergency. He never used it, but it was loud enough to wake the neighborhood!

If your loved one is able to use a telephone, consider installing an extension in his or her room. Twenty-five-foot telephone extension cords are inexpensive and available in most hardware stores. A person with local friends might need a personal telephone line.

Special Furniture and Fixtures

You may need to find a hospital-type bed, if that's what your loved one needs. Paul had become accustomed to this type of bed during his two months in the hospital and his seven months in the nursing home. So first we rented a bed from a medical supply house. Paul's doctor authorized the rental, and Medicare paid some of the cost. Eventually we purchased one.

Why a *hospital* bed for someone who is disabled? This kind of bed is heavy duty, has firm springs, and has a water-repellent mattress. It includes hand cranks that lower or raise the head or the foot of the bed (more expensive models do this electrically). All these are comfort features. The beds may also be ordered with bed rails on both sides; these add to your loved one's security and to the caretaker's peace of mind. If you decide the railings aren't necessary, they can be removed.

If your loved one has trouble getting out of bed, you can rent a "trapeze," a triangular device suspended over and clamped to the bed to assist the person in pulling himself upright. Trapezes are also available with a floor stand and can be used with a chair or a bedside commode. A grab bar next to the bed can also be helpful.

We also had to think about toilet and hygiene needs. We purchased an adjustable-height, self-standing commode for Paul's bedroom, primarily for emergency needs. It had a regular toilet seat and cover, below which was a plastic pail that could be removed easily. In the bathroom I installed railings around the commode as a helpful aid to sitting and rising. An elevated adjustable toilet seat that fits inside your present commode is also helpful—it can increase the seat height up to six inches. Several types are available through medical supply stores.

I also installed a grab bar directly in front of the commode, mounted vertically. Paul could easily reach out and pull himself up to a standing position; later he learned how to pivot his body while holding onto this bar as we prepared for his shower.

Neither Carolyn nor Juanita, our aide, nor I could manage to lift a 185-pounder in and out of a tub. So, at first, we settled on giving Paul showers. I bought a stool that could be placed inside the bathtub, and replaced the shower head with a movable one connected to a plastic hose. This is ideal for shampooing as well as for bathing. Remember that your loved one may not be able to stand or can stand only briefly and with considerable difficulty.

If your loved one feels more comfortable with a bath, you may purchase special plastic chairs, operated by hydraulic water pressure, that allow you to raise or lower him into a bathtub. But these are expensive (several hundred dollars), and your bathroom must be large enough to accommodate this fixture.

It's most important to have a sturdy grab bar in the bathtub. I found one that could be installed horizontally for the entire length of the tub, but there are other options. There are vertical bars which extend from floor to ceiling—but the ceiling must be firm. There are grab bars that can be attached to the bathtub itself. Grab bars are essential to the safety and comfort of someone who bathes or showers but is partially paralyzed, has arthritis, or copes with heart or back problems.

A caution about grab bars—they must be sturdy and firmly affixed to the studs inside your wall. Heavy-duty towel bars will not do. They should be no more than two inches from the wall, so arms will not slide through and cause injury.

Local medical supply stores should have a variety of grab bars and rails and other helpful equipment. You may also try your phone directory under "medical equipment and supplies" or "hospital equipment and supplies." Another excellent source for such items is the Sears *Home Health Care Catalog*. We purchased the hospital bed, the portable commode, and two wheelchairs through Sears.

These kinds of modifications cost money, but expenses can be kept down if you are able to do all or some of the work yourself. I estimate that ramps, the grab bars, the bath handrail, and the portable commode and additional commode units would cost approximately three hundred dollars.

Help through Therapy
It isn't enough just to install equipment. Your loved one must learn to use such facilities properly and safely. Help

is available in teaching your "patient" to manage more efficiently.

Because of Paul's disability we became acquainted with three kinds of therapists—physical, speech, and occupational.

The occupational therapist can help people adjust to home care. He or she can help most handicapped people learn to brush their teeth or clean dentures, shave, bathe, use the commode, dress, pull up their socks, feed themselves, and even do some minor cooking. Paul learned to button his shirt and to operate a zipper with one hand. There are many ingenious tools to help the handicapped—devices for reaching or picking up things, food bumpers that clamp to plates, easy-grip eating utensils, one-hand jar openers, oversize key holders, and devices to safely turn gas on or off.

Discuss your hopes for home care with the occupational therapist. He or she may have important suggestions or modifications for your plans, as well as knowledge and catalogs of suppliers. Once you have decided upon basic modifications and installations, the therapist can work with your loved one to adapt his disability to new surroundings. Occupational therapists like to know the floor plan of your home, and they welcome your participation. They want the disabled person to succeed in his new surroundings. This kind of therapy is available through most hospitals or special clinics; therapists also work with patients in the home.

Mobility with Wheelchairs

I rented a wheelchair for Paul before purchasing one. Then I bought a wheelchair for Anna. You may be surprised at the variety of wheelchairs available. They range in price and style from "Hondas" to "Cadillacs."

Secure professional advice as to the best type of wheelchair for your loved one. Her physical therapist can help. A physiatrist may prescribe a specific kind of wheelchair (and walker) for a disabled or handicapped person. When medically prescribed, insurance coverage may apply. The cost may be deductible for federal income tax purposes.

Wheelchairs come in many shapes and sizes. There are low-slung, lightweight wheelchairs that are used in marathon racing and even in basketball games. There are heavy-duty, battery-operated, motorized units that can turn, reverse, and move forward at 5 m.p.h.

The average utility wheelchair weighs between forty and fifty pounds. Consideration of weight is important if you plan frequent transfer of your patient from wheelchair to car and back. Lifting a heavy folded wheelchair in and out of a car, especially from the trunk, can become a back-breaking activity.

The use of lighter-weight space-age metals has reduced the weight of some models but vastly increased their cost. For occasional transfer use, some families are finding a collapsible *travel chair* useful. It weighs under twenty pounds and folds down much like a child's stroller. You might also consider the *geriatric chair,* which is a high-back cushioned chair with wheels (and brakes), designed for use within a home or building.

If your loved one cannot walk, or walks very little, and will be using a wheelchair most of each day, purchase the sturdiest unit you can afford. Wheelchairs travel many miles. In Anna's nursing home there was a sign that read: "Walkers, 5 m.p.h.—Wheelers, 10 m.p.h." They need to be rugged. Wheelchairs should be sturdy because axles and cross braces break, and wheel bearings wear out. Both Paul's and Anna's chairs were in the shop several times.

Another kind of "wheel-about" chair is designed specifically for transporting people into showers. It is waterproof and rustproof and only practical for use in a shower stall with no outer ledge. Some are designed to double as a bedside commode.

Look for certain things when buying a wheelchair:

- Is the plastic sturdy and washable?
- Are the plastic covers affixed with screws and easily replaceable?
- Are the footrests the swing-away type? Can they be removed? (This is often helpful in transferral to cars or bathtubs.) Are they adjustable in height? (Some can be ordered with heel straps.)
- Are the brakes adjustable and sturdy?
- Does the wheelchair have seatbelts?
- What kind of armrests does it have: full-size and half-size, or "desk-type"? The latter usually is pref-

erable, as it allows a person to get closer to a table or desk. Armrests that are adjustable in height and that are removable allow a person to more easily slide from a chair to bed, for example.

Wheelchairs can be customized, particularly for heavier individuals. Seats come in widths of eighteen, twenty, twenty-two, or twenty-four inches. Specialized wheelchairs are available with higher backs, which can be lowered to a reclining position. Others are designed for amputees; they feature a longer wheelbase for safer balance.

Motorized wheelchairs are battery-operated; the battery must be recharged daily. A fingertip control guides the unit forward, backward, or turns the chair sideways. The motorized wheelchair is heavy and not easily transported, but most are approved for transporting on aircraft, should this be necessary.

Motorized scooters are also available and are helpful in factory and office situations where handicapped persons are employed.

Prices range from three hundred dollars for standard wheelchairs purchased through mail-order houses to six hundred dollars or more through durable medical goods retail stores. Motorized wheelchairs can cost more than three thousand dollars. The motorized scooter sells for approximately twelve hundred dollars.

If your loved one spends a great deal of time in a wheelchair, you might want to buy a cushion for greater comfort and to prevent friction sores.

More on Furniture

The furniture in your home used by a handicapped person should be sturdy. Remember that the disabled often rely on chair arms or tabletops for leverage as they rise or sit down.

Solid armchairs and solid-top tables are preferable. Armless high-backed chairs and drop-leaf tables should be avoided. Rockers are risky, even with arms; if one must be used, place one foot on one of the rocker arches to steady the chair as you assist a handicapped person to sit.

Tables and desks are normally thirty inches high, and most wheelchairs maneuver easily under these. However, drawers or panels can bruise knees. In such cases, you might want to raise the table or desk by placing wooden blocks under the legs. Make sure the blocks are well-secured and the table is not wobbly. Sturdy folding tables can be moved anywhere, indoors or out, and are good surfaces for reading, making handicrafts, or various other activities.

Reducing Your Loved One's Universe

Up to this point, we've been thinking about rearranging *your* home for the care of your loved one. However, the suggestions for safety and comfort apply wherever your loved one is able to continue independent living. If your loved one lives alone, you may want to consider some additional modifications.

Redesign shelves and storage space, putting everything at a lower, safer level. Older people who are not surefooted shouldn't be climbing on ladders or chairs, and many have difficulty reaching for things. Some occupational therapists recommend that kitchen islands be designed to allow a minimum of movement from storage to preparation to partaking of food. The experts also say that "smaller is better," especially in bathrooms. Many older people need walls or solid furniture or fixtures to hold onto in order to maintain balance. Keep this in mind as you rearrange furniture.

Have confidence in your creative imagination as you plan to meet the specific needs of your aging or handicapped loved ones. In deciding what would be helpful in Paul's bathroom and bedroom, I imagined I was paralyzed the way he was. Borrow a wheelchair and wheel yourself through your house, just to see what it's like to traverse the rugs and halls or to negotiate thirty-inch-wide doorways. Check on expandable hinges.

Many older people are fearful of being harassed or robbed. To provide them with greater security and reassurance, install deadbolt locks on front and back doors. These aren't burglar-proof, but they can't be easily jimmied. A chain lock at the front door allows the door to be partially opened for deliveries, but still provides some security. A tiny viewing device can provide a wide-angle, fish-eye view of whoever is outside the door.

Special locks are also available for windows and patio

doors. Walk through the lock section of your hardware store to see what is available and applicable to your loved one's home.

Consider a smoke alarm, and be sure your loved one understands what to do if it is activated. Some of the more sophisticated TV cable systems offer fire and security monitoring on specially assigned channels. Telephone companies are experimenting with similar light-activated sensor services.

An automatic telephone dialing device with memory might be helpful for your loved one. One of the least expensive units provides up to twenty channels for preset calls. He can push a button marked Fire, Police, Doctor, or (Your Name), and put the call through without dialing. Some units provide a "recall key"; if the previous call was busy and did not go through, the unit remembers that number and redials automatically.

Expect the Unexpected
When you decide to provide health care in your home, accept the reality that there *will* be accidents. They will probably be minor, but older people still fall and break bones. Be cautious and take preventive measures, but realize that there are risks in homes *and* institutions.

Your loved one may not make it to the bathroom in time—or get your attention in time. Be prepared to deal with damp or stained rugs. Provide protection to chairs with prized upholstery. Keep a good disinfectant handy for cleaning wheelchairs regularly.

Expect nicks and scratches on furniture from wheelchairs. Walls and door frames will show wear and tear. Expect to use furniture polish, spackling compound, furniture putty, and eventually plaster and paint. You might want to install metal or wooden protectors for well-trafficked exposed corners.

If we are to provide a loving and caring environment for *people,* we will have to risk some loss and damage to *things.*

4
When Nursing Home Care Becomes Necessary

Nursing homes have had bad press coverage—sometimes deservedly so. The nursing home industry in the United States is big business. One chain owns more than a thousand homes. That isn't an evil by itself but size and profit motive do not necessarily guarantee quality care.

There have been abuses in nursing homes. Health department standards have not always been followed. Too often inspections are known in advance and become a farce. Residents have been "warehoused"—oversedated, under-monitored, and moved about within the facility for the convenience of the institution rather than the comfort and sense of security of the resident. Too often nursing home staff are poorly trained, poorly motivated, and poorly paid. And, too often, this is the image that caregivers have of a nursing home.

Our loved ones have another image, equally unpleasant—that of the county "old people's home" or "poor house." When some elderly persons adamantly insist they will never live in a nursing home, they are responding to their horror and fear of an image that originated in their youth.

Correction of both images is needed.

Nursing Homes Are Necessary

Nursing homes are required to provide *intermediate* care (usually short-term, with limited medical attention) and *skilled* care (usually long-term, with around-the-clock medical attention). There are excellent, good, mediocre, and poor nursing homes. Much can be done to improve the quality and level of care even in the best of facilities.

If nursing homes didn't exist, we'd have to invent them. More than a million Americans now reside in such facilities. A small percentage of them could probably be served better in other ways, but the vast majority do need and require special care comparable to hospital care, which nursing homes provide at far less cost.

I can affirm that nursing homes exist to meet the medical needs of a large group of chronically ill people as economically as possible. No one is admitted to a nursing home without a physician's order. No one transfers from one nursing home to another without a physician's knowledge and concurrence. Nursing homes specialize in providing medication and treatments, supervising diets, charting and recordkeeping, maintaining cleanliness, and organizing activities. They are neither rest homes nor retirement centers; if they are chosen for either purpose, someone has made a poor choice.

When you and your physician become aware of severe mental loss in your loved one, apart from more obvious physical disabilities, it may be time to seriously consider selecting a nursing home.

How to Select a Nursing Home

When your physician recommends a nursing home for your loved one, where do you begin? What do you do?

Your doctor will likely provide you with names of several facilities. If he treats elderly people, he visits nursing homes with some regularity. If you ask for recommendations, your doctor will level with you. Physicians know where quality care exists.

Check your telephone directory for additional leads. Ask your pastor about church-owned facilities in your area.

Do some preliminary screening by telephone. Your doctor has told you what level of care is required. Ask if the facility provides this and whether there are vacancies.

Once you have narrowed your list, check with the Better

Business Bureau to determine whether all are reputable facilities.

Then investigate the nursing homes for yourself. Take your time to observe and ask questions. Don't be rushed into making a decision.

A Checklist

The following checklist was prepared by HEW, now reorganized as the Department of Health and Human Services (HHS). The list will help you to ask some of the right questions when you visit a nursing home.

	Yes	No
1. Does the home have a current license from the state?	___	___
2. Does the administrator have a current license from the state?	___	___
3. If you need and are eligible for financial assistance, is the home certified to participate in government or other programs that provide it?	___	___
4. Does the home provide special services such as a specific diet or therapy which the patient needs?	___	___
5. Location:		
a) Pleasing to the patient?	___	___
b) Convenient for patient's personal doctor?	___	___
c) Convenient for frequent visitors?	___	___
d) Near a hospital?	___	___

6. Accident prevention:
   a) Well-lighted inside? ___ ___
   b) Free of hazards underfoot? ___ ___
   c) Chairs sturdy and not easily tipped? ___ ___
   d) Warning signs posted around freshly
      waxed floors? ___ ___
   e) Handrails in hallways and grab bars in
      bathrooms? ___ ___
7. Fire safety:
   a) Meets federal and state codes? ___ ___
   b) Exits clearly marked and unobstructed? ___ ___
   c) Written emergency evacuation plan? ___ ___
   d) Frequent fire drills? ___ ___
   e) Exit doors not locked on the inside? ___ ___
   f) Stairways enclosed and doors to stair-
      ways kept closed? ___ ___
8. Bedrooms:
   a) Open into hall? ___ ___
   b) Window? ___ ___
   c) No more than four beds per room? ___ ___
   d) Easy access to each bed? ___ ___
   e) Drapery for each bed? ___ ___
   f) Nurse call bell by each bed? ___ ___
   g) Fresh drinking water at each bed? ___ ___
   h) At least one comfortable chair for each
      patient? ___ ___
   i) Reading lights? ___ ___
   j) Clothes closet and drawers? ___ ___
   k) Room for a wheelchair to maneuver? ___ ___

    l) Care in selecting roommates?   ___ __

9. Cleanliness:

    a) Generally clean, even though it may have a lived-in look?   ___ __

    b) Free of unpleasant odors?   ___ __

    c) Incontinent patients given prompt attention?   ___ __

10. Lobby:

    a) Is the atmosphere welcoming?   ___ __

    b) If also a lounge, is it being used by residents?   ___ __

    c) Furniture attractive and comfortable?   ___ __

    d) Plants and flowers?   ___ __

    e) Certificates and licenses on display?   ___ __

11. Hallways:

    a) Large enough for two wheelchairs to pass with ease?   ___ __

    b) Hand-grip railings on the sides?   ___ __

12. Dining room:

    a) Attractive and inviting?   ___ __

    b) Comfortable chairs and tables?   ___ __

    c) Easy to move around in?   ___ __

    d) Tables convenient for those in wheelchairs set?   ___ __

    e) Food tasty and attractively served?   ___ __

    f) Meals match posted menu?   ___ __

    g) Those needing help receiving it?   ___ __

13. Kitchen:

    a) Food preparation, dishwashing, and garbage areas separated?   ___ __

    b) Food needing refrigeration not standing on counters? _____ _____

    c) Kitchen help observe sanitation rules? _____ _____

14. Activity rooms:

    a) Rooms available for patients' activities? _____ _____

    b) Equipment (such as games, easels, yarn, kiln) available? _____ _____

    c) Patients using equipment? _____ _____

15. Special-purpose rooms:

    a) Rooms set aside for physical examinations or therapy? _____ _____

    b) Rooms being used for stated purpose? _____ _____

16. Isolation room:

    a) At least one bed and bathroom available for patients with contagious illness? _____ _____

17. Toilet facilities:

    a) Convenient to bedrooms? _____ _____

    b) Easy for wheelchair patient to use? _____ _____

    c) Sink? _____ _____

    d) Nurse call bell? _____ _____

    e) Hand grips on or near toilets? _____ _____

    f) Bathtubs and showers with nonslip surfaces? _____ _____

18. Grounds:

    a) Residents can get fresh air? _____ _____

    b) Ramps to help handicapped? _____ _____

19. Medical:

    a) Physician available in emergency? _____ _____

    b) Private physician allowed? _____ _____

    c) Regular medical attention assured?   __ __

    d) Thorough physical immediately before
        or upon admission?   __ __

    e) Medical records and plan of care kept?   __ __

    f) Patient involved in developing plans
        for treatment?   __ __

    g) Other medical services (dentists,
        optometrists, etc.) available regularly?   __ __

    h) Freedom to purchase medicines
        outside home?   __ __

20. Hospitalization:

    a) Arrangement with nearby hospital for
        transfer when necessary?   __ __

21. Nursing services:

    a) R.N. responsible for nursing staff in a
        skilled nursing home?   __ __

    b) L.P.N. on duty day and night in a
        skilled nursing home?   __ __

    c) Trained nurses' aides and orderlies on
        duty in homes providing some nursing
        care?   __ __

22. Rehabilitation:

    a) Specialists in various therapies available
        when needed?   __ __

23. Activities program:

    a) Individual patient preferences observed? __ __

    b) Group and individual activities?   __ __

    c) Residents encouraged but not forced to
        participate?   __ __

d) Outside trips for those who can go? ___ ___

e) Volunteers from the community work
with the patients? ___ ___

24. Religious observances:

a) Arrangements made for patient to
worship as he pleases? ___ ___

b) Religious observances a matter of
choice? ___ ___

25. Social services:

a) Social worker available to help residents
and families? ___ ___

26. Food:

a) Dietitian plans menus for patients on
special diets? ___ ___

b) Variety from meal to meal? ___ ___

c) Meals served at normal times? ___ ___

d) Plenty of time for each meal? ___ ___

e) Snacks? ___ ___

f) Food delivered to patients' rooms? ___ ___

g) Help with eating given when needed? ___ ___

27. Grooming:

a) Barbers and beauticians available for
men and women? ___ ___

28. General atmosphere friendly and
supportive? ___ ___

29. Residents retain human rights? ___ ___

a) May participate in planning treatment? ___ ___

b) Medical records kept confidential? ___ ___

c) Can veto experimental research? ___ ___

d) Have freedom and privacy to attend to personal needs?   ___ ___

e) Married couples may share room?   ___ ___

f) All have opportunities to socialize?   ___ ___

g) May manage own finances if capable, or obtain accounting if not?   ___ ___

h) May decorate own bedrooms?   ___ ___

i) May wear own clothes?   ___ ___

j) May communicate with anyone without censorship?   ___ ___

k) Are not transferred or discharged arbitrarily?   ___ ___

30. Administrator and staff available to discuss problems?   ___ ___

a) Patients and relatives can discuss complaints without fear of reprisal?   ___ ___

b) Staff responds to calls quickly and courteously?   ___ ___

31. Residents appear alert unless very ill?   ___ ___

32. Visiting hours accommodate residents and relatives?   ___ ___

33. Civil rights regulations observed?   ___ ___

34. Visitors and volunteers pleased with home?   ___ ___

Caveat Emptor—"Let the Buyer Beware"

Here are additional questions to consider:

Is the facility both Medicare and Medicaid approved? Medicare is available to anyone receiving Social Security;

its benefits for nursing home care are limited but its requirements are more stringent (thus some nursing homes will not accept Medicare patients).

What other insurance plans are accepted by the facility?

Is a charge made for doing personal laundry? May relatives handle this chore if they choose?

Is there a resident or "on call" physician?

What arrangements can be made for therapy? At what cost?

What limitations are there for personal items in the room—for example, a favorite chair, an extra chest of drawers, or a TV set? Can pictures be hung on the walls?

Are there restrictions on making or receiving telephone calls? Is a private telephone allowed?

Where is the resident's personal money kept? Your loved one will need some spending money for incidentals often available in the home and for offerings. If your loved one cannot handle cash, have a small discretionary "trust" fund set up with the bookkeeper to pay for haircuts, Beauty Shop, and other small purchases.

When was the facility last inspected by the appropriate city and state authorities?

Does the facility have a sprinkler system? How does the facility interpret "fire drill"? What special training is given to staff for such emergencies?

What are the regulations regarding smoking? Is it allowed in the dining room or in the residents' rooms? Is the staff allowed to smoke at desks or nursing stations?

Or is smoking restricted to certain areas? Smoking regulations not only affect patients and visitors with respiratory ailments but fire safety as well.

Probe a bit about the work of the activities director. Ask to see a list of the preceding month's activities. Is there an active volunteer group or auxiliary?

Is there a resident chaplain, or a local pastor who regularly visits the facility? Is this permitted? What religious services or Bible classes are held or allowed?

Ask to see the menus for the past several days. Is a daily menu posted for residents to see? Observe the serving of a noon meal—usually the biggest meal of the day. What provision is made for special diets or preferences? Is there ample variety of the primary food groups? Is the food prepared and served attractively?

Find Out Who's in Charge

Since the welfare of your loved one is involved, don't ever feel inhibited about asking questions. Carolyn and I have visited more than a dozen nursing homes, and the best ones will always welcome your questions, give you all the time you want or need, take you anywhere within the facility, and will not pressure you for an immediate decision. In fact, the better facilities welcome a return visit—with your loved one if possible—so that other questions can be raised and answered before a final joint decision is made.

If you are ever made to feel that you are intruding or meddling with your questions, then leave right away. Since you will likely be entering a relationship of considerable duration, mutual trust and rapport must be established quickly if these are to flourish and continue.

Try to see the administrator. He or she may not be able to give you all the time you need or want at that particular time, but you must make contact with the person in charge. Check to see if his or her license and other qualifications are prominently displayed. You must have an opportunity to evaluate the style and character of the person who sets the tone for the entire facility. Something is wrong with management if the chief administrator is always absent or seems reluctant to meet the public.

Experienced nursing home staff will tell you that adjustment to the nursing home environment usually takes three months. These are the crucial weeks during which you must have a good working relationship with the administrator, not merely with a subordinate. You will have new questions to ask about procedure. You may have complaints. It's better for staff morale and for your loved one's well-being if you are free to go to the top to find answers and solutions.

Evaluate Nonprofit Facilities First

In your search for a nursing home, look first at church-related or other nonprofit facilities, if they exist in your area. Nonprofit homes tend to have larger staffs and more extensive programs. Church-related facilities offer a dimension of "tender loving care" that commercial enterprises often don't.

Investigate Performance Expectations

Good nursing homes have high standards of performance and conduct for their staff. They provide training and orientation for newly employed staff and continuing education for all staff members.

One nursing home has the following paragraph in its statement of personnel policies and procedures.

> The patient comes first. The patient is not an interruption of our work; he is the purpose of it. The patient is not someone with whom to argue or match wits. He is an important individual having feelings, emotions, prejudices, and wants. It is not only our job to care for his needs, but to contribute in every way to his comfort and happiness.

This same nursing home fires employees for "soliciting or accepting tips" and for "physical or verbal abuse of patients." That kind of policy builds confidence.

Become Familiar with Residents' Rights

Nursing homes are required to provide new residents with a list of "patient's rights." Ask to see a copy. Here are a few examples of those rights.

- The patient is fully informed, by a physician, of his medical condition.
- He may participate in the planning of his medical treatment.

- The patient is transferred or discharged only for medical reasons.
- The patient is free from mental and physical abuse, and free from chemical and non-emergency physical restraints, except as authorized in writing by a physician for a specified and limited period of time, or when necessary to protect the patient from injury to himself or to others.
- He is treated with consideration, respect, and full recognition of his dignity and individuality, including privacy in treatment and in care for his personal needs.
- If married, the patient is assured privacy for visits by his or her spouse; if both are patients in the facility, they are permitted to share a room.

The Need to Monitor Nursing Home Care

Since policy is not always implemented, what can we do to insure continuing good care for our loved ones in nursing homes?

There is no substitute for personal observation and visits. Observe the operation of the facility at different times of the day and week, with different staff on different shifts. Once you are recognized as the responsible person who is interested in your relative, it becomes easier to resolve problems.

You need to see your loved one at different times of the day. If emotional or physical needs are not being met, this may cause your loved one to become withdrawn or actively abusive.

Anna had difficulty with roommates during her first three months of nursing home residence. Her first companion emptied her dresser drawers as often as Anna did, and the mix-up of personal belongings brought them to literal blows. Her second suffered from kleptomania. Anna's things kept disappearing—including her glasses and even her false teeth! Nursing homes try to put compatible people together, but the process takes time. You need to be aware of what is going on.

The quality of care and food must be monitored. There may be occasion to complain or to raise questions. However, your visits with administrative and supervisory staff ought not to be limited just to complaining. The more you visit the facility, the more you will wonder how the staff copes as well as it does. A little affirmation and commendation goes a long way; there is little of it from patients, and not a great deal from patients' relatives.

Some of the better nursing home facilities plan for regular "family meetings," held at least quarterly, where senior staff, relatives, and patients (if they wish to or can attend) meet together to share news and concerns, to raise questions about procedures, or to suggest new programs or developments.

A few nursing homes have organized "resident councils" in which residents participate in some of the decision-making that affects their lives. There are physical limitations to such participation, but it is both good strategy and good management when such joint planning is allowed to happen.

Improving the Nursing Home "Community"

The nursing home environment can be improved; constructive suggestions can be made to management at family meetings or resident councils. Here are several ideas to ponder, whether you are choosing a home or trying to improve the one where your loved one lives. Some ideas may only need *your* time and energy to implement.

1. *Pay the aides more money.* The people who do most of the work in nursing homes are the least educated, the least skilled, and the least paid. On-the-job training will help. However, standards won't be raised until wages rise. Higher pay scales might also help decrease the high turnover rate of nursing home employees.

2. *Provide patients with more sunshine and fresh air.* Safe patio areas can be added or incorporated with plans for new construction. Exits and entrances should be designed for ease of movement of handicapped persons; lighter-weight doors might be used. Aides or volunteers could assist residents with a bit of walking, or pushing a wheelchair outdoors, and returning the patient indoors. On warmer days it would be a lot healthier for residents to sit in the sun than around the nurses' station.

I know of one nursing home that built a lovely fenced-in patio and equipped it with weatherproof furniture. But it was never used. The patio was accessible only through a gate outside the building; the architects forgot to include a doorway from inside the facility.

3. *Be creative with color.* Paint costs about the same, whether it's white or blue or orange or green. Many psychological studies, developed especially for industry, prove that certain colors are more restful than others. The drabness of nursing home facilities could be corrected with color, including wallpaper. Varying the colors of rooms and corridors might help those patients who aren't color-blind find their hallway and their rooms more easily. Such color-coding can help both residents and staff.

4. *Provide nutritious snacks between meals.* Finger foods help digestion and might even reduce the need for daily laxatives. Carrot and celery sticks, slices of apple, or other fruits and vegetables can help. It would take more time and perhaps more staff, but better health would result.

Usually raw vegetables and fresh fruit must be prepared so a patient can eat these and benefit from them; giving an apple or an orange to a patient who is partially paralyzed, who suffers from arthritis, or who wears loose dentures won't get this good food eaten.

5. *Add a bit of beauty.* Posters and paintings dress up hallways and walls. They also provide "landmarks" as residents move through the facility. Large photomurals or scenic color panels printed as wallpaper can provide new "windows" in some of the larger rooms. Individual wall hangings could be placed behind or beside each bed to

add beauty and individuality. It might be a simple framed picture, some needlepoint, or even something woven. Plants add life and color.

Flower boxes on patios would brighten the area. Perhaps some of the residents could plant the seeds. It's exciting to watch things grow.

An aviary on a patio would require someone's special care and attention, but the color and sound of birds would brighten many lives. So would a small aquarium in the lobby or lounge of the nursing facility. Bird feeders and bird baths attract feathered friends if someone keeps them filled with seed and water.

I often wish that pets were allowed in nursing homes, so patients could have something warm and cuddly to love. But at least we could arrange more pet shows. Children enjoy parading their pets, and residents enjoy a show-and-tell-and-touch time. I took Rascal, our German Shepherd, to Paul's nursing home a few times—keeping her outdoors, of course. Rascal's cavorting brought smiles to many faces.

6. *Alter schedules to benefit the residents, not the staff.* Nursing homes operate much as hospitals do. Patients are awakened at 7:00 A.M. or even earlier. Often the staff begins serving the evening meal as early as 4:30 P.M. and patients are put to bed by 7:30 or 8:00. Why should it be so? They aren't young children! There's lots of good television to be seen between 7:00 and 10:00 P.M.; such TV programs are important windows on the world for people who need all the "reality orientation" they can get.

It shouldn't be denied them because of institutional dictum or tradition. Let people live while they live.

7. *Provide more living space.* Because construction costs are so high, space is costly. But only with adequate space can nursing homes truly be *homes.* Many smaller nursing homes being built today do not allow for enough public rooms. There isn't much opportunity for movement or group interaction when dining rooms double as activity rooms, and lobbies (often facing administrative offices) are the only lounges. I'm convinced that the lack of adequate "public space" accounts for much of the crowding of hallways and areas facing nurses' stations.

When building a new nursing home—or in modifying an older one—why not plan for *several* smaller rooms for activities? One could be used for sewing, another for crafts; disarray could be overlooked because these would be rooms for ongoing creative activity. Another room might be set aside for playing games. There might be *two* television viewing rooms in order to have at least two choices of channel.

A larger multi-purpose room could be used for group exercises, programs, staff and resident council meetings, and resident talent shows. This larger room might also serve as the home's worship center. It should not be the dining room, where cooking odors permeate the air and kitchen staff are busy preparing food and setting tables.

Architects need to pay more attention to the requirements of audio-visuals. They do this when designing schools and churches, so why not nursing homes? Films have proven their educational value; yet it is often impossible to darken the public rooms of nursing homes to show a movie or slides during daylight hours.

8. *Engineer better climate control.* Most of the newer facilities are air-conditioned. Some use individual heat-pump units similar to those found in motels. These can be regulated to suit individual preferences. However, sometimes handicapped or disoriented people either won't bother or are unable to work the controls—or they will change them compulsively and erratically.

The slower metabolism of older people makes them more susceptible to extreme changes of heat or cold without their showing the normal signs of sweating or shivering. And because they move about less, they often need a higher room temperature to survive. Hypothermia (dangerously low body temperature) is more of a risk for persons past 65. A consistent temperature ought to be maintained.

Blankets should be used at night. Most often a patient is covered only by a sheet or perhaps a bedspread. I suspect this is done because sheets and bedspreads are easier to launder than blankets. Again, this procedure is based upon the convenience of the institution rather than upon the patient's needs. I've seen many nursing home residents huddled up because they are cold. Lightweight thermal blankets might be an economical answer.

9. *Provide opportunities for learning.* Older people can and want to learn new things. Some may want to wrestle with the ideas of a new book. Others would enjoy serious

Bible study. Classes such as these could bring an exciting dimension of growth to nursing home residents.

10. *Discover ways for residents to share with others.* The need to share is part of what keeps us human and caring.

Nursing home patients do not have much discretionary income; most are no longer able to contribute money to causes they would like to support or have supported in the past.

But there are other ways to share. They can serve as volunteers. They can sew or make simple toys for needy children at Christmastime. They can prepare mailings for the United Way or some other local charity. Rock-a-thons (similar to Walk-a-thons, but using rockers instead of feet) can be organized to benefit the Heart Fund or other charities. Some residents adopt another more handicapped resident in the same home and find ways to be helpful.

A nursing home in Minnesota operates a day-care center for children in its facilities. Residents serve as honorary grandparents and are especially helpful with the very young. This interaction meets the needs of two generations.

11. *Incorporate more opportunities for spiritual involvement.* This is especially important for secular, commercial nursing homes to remember. Neighborhood churches can be enlisted to provide worship services. A retired pastor might serve as voluntary chaplain—with a regular visitation schedule and perhaps a weekly Bible class.

Let music be part of the environment. Church and

school choirs, children's choirs, and handbell choirs might provide mini-concerts. Hymn sings are always popular. Sacred, classical, or soothing popular music (most residents would remember music from the forties) could be played over the public address system.

Opportunities for spiritual involvement could include many cultural programs. Local musicians could give concerts—one classical pianist received a federal arts grant to do just this in her city. High-school groups might present occasional plays. Barbershop quartets would provide lots of fun and stir up happy memories.

12. *Consistently practice the principle of "team assessment."* This is an opportunity for all the staff—medical and social—to evaluate the progress and/or problems of individual patients. The activities director may have observed an attitude or a symptom the director of nursing needs to know about. The food services director (or dining-room monitor) may have important impressions and information to share. Solutions to problems can be sought and tried out, and serious commitment to rehabilitation can be demonstrated. Nursing homes need the services of professional social workers, full- or part-time, to assist the institutional team and to help patients and their families.

Many nursing homes already have incorporated several of these suggestions to provide more professional and more stimulating care.

Residents of nursing homes have a variety of needs, which family members and volunteers can help the staff to meet. Volunteers could lighten staff workers' burdens by assisting communication with residents and their families, enhancing creativity, teaching new crafts, developing a sense of community and self-worth among the residents, and providing time and an environment for contemplation and worship. They can bring cheer to cheerless lives.

5
What about Professional Medical Care?

$\mathbf{A}$ reliable and readily available family physician is an essential requirement, not only for your family but also for those older persons for whom you are responsible.

Since medical practices have changed radically over the past few years, securing appropriate and adequate medical help is a greater problem than it once was. The medical clinic or complex has emerged; specialization has increased. It has become difficult to know where and to whom to turn.

Questions to Ask
In our search for medical care for Anna and Paul, I asked these questions:

Would my present family physician accept an additional patient? Many physicians today are overloaded and are turning down new patients, so don't assume your doctor will be willing to care for your loved one—ask.

Would my family physician accept an older patient? Does he or she have experience in geriatric medicine?

People joke about house calls, but find out if your physician still makes them. Emergencies arise, and it isn't always possible to get a loved one to the doctor's office; besides, illnesses don't always coincide with established office hours. Find out whether your physician makes calls to nursing homes; if so, to which ones; if not, would he do so? Fortunately, our family doctor accepted new patients, treated older people, made calls to nursing homes, and came to our home in an emergency.

Ask your doctor how he plans to monitor the medical care of your loved one in a nursing home. Professional staff within the nursing home must be consulted, of course, but a physician should not rely only on that one source of information.

When you locate a physician for your loved one, ask if he would prescribe generic brand drugs instead of the more expensive brand-name drugs, which are often produced by the same manufacturer.

Finding a Physician

If your present family physician can't or won't accept an additional patient, you will need to find someone who will. This person ought to be a general practitioner or someone active in "family practice" or "geriatric medicine" (categories you'll find in the Yellow Pages under "physicians and surgeons").

Begin with the telephone directory and the local medical association. Ask some of your older retired friends whom they see about their medical problems. Doctors have reputations for empathy or for brusqueness, for caring or for cold professionalism. If possible, arrange for a personal interview.

You are shopping for competence, compassion, and continuity. Find out whether the doctor plans an early retirement. This might make a difference in your plans. Although a physician's professional ability and skill are not necessarily related to his or her faith, I appreciate a capable physician who is also a person of faith. Our family physician is a member of the church we attend. My urologist, who was also Paul's, paused to pray before beginning an operation. The rapport that grows out of mutual respect of God's power goes beyond any immediate medical problem.

Special Medical People
We found we needed specialists for special needs. Your regular family doctor will make recommendations as needed for specialists you have to consult.

I had never heard of a physiatrist until Paul had his stroke, or CVA (cerebrovascular accident). A physiatrist specializes in physical medicine and rehabilitation, including muscular movement. This science grew out of recent wars, when severely wounded and disabled veterans required special care and rehabilitation. While it is still a developing science, its lessons and procedures are helping countless accident (including burn) victims of all ages.

Physiatrists prescribe the type, kind, and length of therapies that are carried out by physical, occupational, and speech therapists. Older persons with stroke or heart problems, or those with muscular or arthritic difficulties, benefit from such specialized help.

We also needed a urologist. Many older males develop prostate problems—my father died of prostate cancer. Urinary-tract or kidney infections have replaced pulmonary infections as a leading cause of death among the elderly, both male and female. We also needed to find a dermatologist (a skin specialist). Our family physician was suspicious of a discoloration on Paul's scalp; it turned out to be malignant. A dermatologist successfully treated Paul as an outpatient. Dermatologists also help in treating fungus, dry skin conditions (especially bothersome to older people during colder months), and athlete's foot. They remove warts and other surface growths.

Anna required a neurologist to diagnose the status of her brain and nervous system. Neurologists give CAT scans, as well as the newer "image resonance" scans. Later, Anna needed an orthopedic surgeon to repair her broken hip.

Hearing may have to be checked and impacted wax removed. Some doctors still specialize in ear, nose, and throat disorders. Otologists are ear specialists.

Eyes deteriorate with age and should be tested regularly. Glaucoma is a special risk for the elderly. An optometrist examines eyes for vision and prescribes glasses. An opthalmologist also examines eyes and prescribes glasses, but he is a medical doctor who can diagnose and treat diseases of the eye and perform surgery. An optician fills prescriptions and grinds lenses for glasses.

Dental Needs

Older people's teeth or dentures should be checked, cleaned, and maintained regularly. Some dentists make visits to nursing homes, bringing portable equipment for routine maintenance of teeth and dentures or for making molds for new dentures.

Medical Transportation

It may not be necessary for your loved one who lives in a nursing home to leave the facility for medical treatment. Physicians are expected to visit nursing home patients. In fact, Medicaid patients are to be visited *monthly*. Although nursing homes do not have X-ray equipment, portable mobile X-ray units can be summoned as needed. At a physician's request, laboratories will also send technicians to the nursing home (or to your home) for blood and specimen tests.

Ambulances cost fifty dollars or more per trip within city limits. If your doctor believes an emergency requires an ambulance, by all means call an ambulance service, and agree to do this quickly if the nursing home calls you. However, for routine visits to doctors or dentists, drive your loved one yourself. It's probably more reassuring, and it is obviously more economical. Some cities also provide "medicabs" or minibusses for handicapped people.

Other Forms of Medical Care

There may be times when you'll need a registered nurse (R.N.) or licensed practical nurse (L.P.N.), but often an experienced paramedic or nurse's aide can provide the special health care required. Consult your public health agency or a professional referral service. The next chapter offers suggestions about hiring such help.

However, medical care as such may not always be needed. Handicapped people aren't sick—they're handicapped. Disoriented people aren't ill—they're merely confused. Perhaps only a companion or a "sitter" is required.

Whatever the physical state of your loved one, you'll feel more secure and competent about home health care if you take time to learn the basics. Books and guides may be purchased at your bookstore or borrowed from your public library. The Red Cross periodically offers courses in first aid and in home health care.

The techniques of turning, bathing, and changing bed linens of patients in bed are skills that can be learned and used in many different kinds of situations. And when medical help is needed, it's available in quantity and quality. Today we are very blessed.

6
Hiring for Home Health Care

Carolyn and I soon realized that we and others of our family who lived in Austin could not care for Anna (and later, for Paul) all by ourselves. We had to find help.

When you arrive at that point, remember that there are many different ways of caring for invalid or handicapped loved ones at home. They are costly, but take time to compare these costs with those of nursing homes.

When husband and wife both work outside the home, someone needs to be at home to be the caretaker and caregiver. Even when only one spouse leaves home to work, the other needs time off from health care for home care. And both spouses need time off for themselves. Recognize that the decision to provide home care for a loved one literally means providing twenty-four-hour-a-day care. I'll return to this point later.

Levels of Care

Except in severe illnesses, a *full-time registered nurse* will not be required. In such cases, a hospital or a skilled nursing facility ought to be considered. For occasional medical needs, such as giving injections or other medication, special arrangements can be made with a private R.N., a nursing service agency, or the public health program in your area.

Frequently, an L.P.N. (*Licensed Practical Nurse*) or L.V.N. (*Licensed Vocational Nurse*) can perform many of the same medical services at a lower hourly rate. Another less expensive alternative, when patients do not require frequent medical attention, is to hire a *nurse's aide*—a paramedical person trained in providing more limited care for handicapped and bedridden persons. Aides can cope with the special requirements of patient hygiene, check blood pressure, give enemas, exercise muscles, and assist a handicapped person in walking. Aides do not give injections, but they are permitted to administer other medication on schedule.

If no serious medical problems exist but your loved one is basically disoriented and confused, you might hire an adult sitter or companion.

These four types of help can be hired through professional medical employment agencies or pools. Look for them under the "nurses' registries" category in your telephone book. Hiring a person through an agency will cost more per hour, but eliminates the need for handling the detailed paperwork of withholding taxes and Social Security.

For those with limited financial resources, reimbursement for some of these services—including homemaker or "chore care" services—may be available through your welfare agency.

Therapists

Physical, occupational, and speech therapists may be hired on a per-visit basis in your home—or you can arrange to transport your loved one to clinics established for this purpose. Mental health centers sometimes provide therapists through outreach programs.

Your Accountability to the Federal Government

If you decide not to hire someone through an agency, prepare yourself for some bookkeeping tasks. First, apply to the Internal Revenue Service for an "employer identification number." This can be in your name or in your loved one's name. (I chose to apply in Paul's name.)

Your employee must fill out a W-4 form upon being hired, indicating Social Security number and the number of exemptions claimed. File these forms; they authorize you to make deductions for withholding taxes. As an employer, you share in Social Security payments; obtain current schedules from the IRS or your local Social Security office.

You must file quarterly statements with the IRS, remitting the tax money you have withheld. Your remittance to the IRS should include both withholding taxes and Social Security (your employee's and your portion). You will make an annual report to the Social Security Administration on the total amount you sent during the year through the IRS.

Practical Considerations: Pay and Expectations

You'll want to pay at least the minimum hourly wage. You may have to match what the employee would receive through a nursing pool or agency (not what you pay the agency, which then makes its own deductions). You'll need to agree on payments for overtime or holidays, if you expect this from your employee, and to determine the amount of sick leave and vacation time and how often you will consider periodic pay increases.

In evaluating a potential employee, determine your own criteria. Consider such things as experience, compatibility (both with your loved one and your family), empathy with older people, personal habits and appearance, ability to drive, willingness to cook occasionally, ability to read out loud with enjoyment, and some interest in hobbies.

An Example: Juanita

Juanita Sanders was an answer to our prayers. She enjoyed older people. She and Paul hit it off immediately; they both spoke Spanish as well as English. Juanita was a careful driver; she took Paul in hid old Dodge to the rehabilitation clinic for therapy and later to a day activities center two or three times a week.

Juanita was interested in what the various therapists were doing; she wanted to improve her skills for future cases, so what she observed she practiced at home with Paul. She was excited about the exercises demonstrated at the activities center. She followed through with these at home, besides walking daily with Paul.

She took pride in Paul's appearance. His daily shave and shower became a ritual. She knew he liked to wear a tie with his shirt so she always made sure he had one on. She recognized his need for personal dignity.

She practiced what she heard and saw of speech therapy. We chuckled at some of her pronunciations, but she meant well and she loved to read to Paul. She read the Bible in English and Spanish; Paul would usually point to the passage he wanted read. They also read books together. In time, she made a profession of faith, largely due to the things she had read to Paul.

Juanita was not only a good nurse's aide; she was also a responsible companion. When it seemed possible and feasible for Paul to travel to Florida for a Christmas reunion with his two brothers and sister, we had no qualms about Juanita accompanying him on the plane and caring for him in Florida.

As Juanita approached her retirement, she became ill. Because of the commitments Carolyn and I both had at that time, we moved Paul into a nursing home for one month. Paul understood that it was a short-term arrangement and a respite for Juanita and for us, and he cooperated fully.

Then Juanita discovered she would need surgery. Because she was a diabetic, her doctor wanted to avoid an operation. Finally he insisted she find a "lighter" case. Reluctantly, we all agreed to part.

During the next twelve weeks we had three substitutes. Carolyn and I alternated working full-time at home, exhausting our own sick leave. We could not find a suitable new aide and companion, and now we had become worn out. The time had come to find an alternative. Paul shared in the decision to find a good nursing home.

It's Your Time and Your Home

Home care is a glorious proposition, but it is costly—in dollars and cents, and in energy and life-style.

When you add up everything you pay for a visiting R.N. or L.P.N., plus wages for a nurse's aide or companion, your monthly total will probably equal or surpass what nursing home care would cost. Saving money, of course, isn't the reason you may opt for home care.

Remember that there are 168 hours in a week. At most, you will hire someone during the daytime hours—perhaps for 45 hours a week. That leaves 123 hours per week for which you are responsible, in addition to your own regular work at home or away from home.

Many of those hours will be night-time hours, usually occupied with sleep. But Carolyn and I, who chose home care for nearly four years, can testify that very few nights are filled with total, peaceful slumber—much like the nights when we cared for our children as newborns. Only now we were conscious of moans and groans instead of childish wails. We got up often to check on whether a parent was covered, a catheter was still attached, or a parent was still breathing.

Paul shared breakfast with us, which meant that we woke him and got him up. Juanita arrived during breakfast. Usually all of us were back home in time to share supper together. Our weekends were given over entirely to Paul's care, as we did the things Juanita did Monday through Friday.

And of course, Carolyn or I put Paul to bed every night, except for those weekends when we slipped away. We learned we had to take respite breaks once every six or seven weeks.

Perhaps this sounds like martyrdom. It wasn't. We chose to do what we did. We were glad we were able to involve our lives with Paul in this way. We were often tired and frustrated, but we sensed more of the sweet than we did of the bitter.

I must emphasize that the decision to provide home care must be a careful decision to commit yourself, your mate, and any children still living at home to caring for your loved one.

Unless you are able to afford around-the-clock help, you will be responsible for two-thirds of every week. This will affect all your relationships, inside and outside the home. It will affect activities, hobbies, and leisure time.

It will affect other members of the family and your marriage.

Dr. Rita Rogers described some of this at the 1980 meeting of the American Psychiatric Association. She said that it takes a mature partner in a healthy marriage to accept the situation and provide the necessary support and comfort. Old rivalries among children are often revived when it's time to care for an elderly parent. The question of which child the parent liked best may resurface. Spanning these tensions is the impact of time and the physical presence of another adult.

You will have to decide whether home care is the best way for you to go. We believed it was the preferred alternative for us. It was best for Anna as long as she was able to cope with semi-independent living. It was excellent for Paul, because only in this way was he able to benefit from the three kinds of therapy that equipped him for limited independence in a fine nursing home.

Home care takes its toll of energy. It rewards you, however, with renewed relationships with loved ones and the discovery of the nature of compassion. You may not always be ecstatic or enthusiastic about this new relationship, but you will be enormously satisfied.

7
Transporting Your Handicapped Loved One

Whether your handicapped loved one lives with you or in a nursing home facility, there will be times when you want to go out for a drive. You may need to visit a doctor or dentist, and transportation becomes a necessity. Other times, the trip is for a change of scene and pace— shopping, a meal out, or some celebration or excursion.

Transporting a handicapped loved one isn't difficult, but it is different from anything you may have experienced previously. You need to be aware of these differences so you can plan ahead and overcome your understandable hesitancy and fear. Soon you will realize that in this area, too, "practice makes perfect"—or at least it will make things more comfortable for both you and your loved one.

I still shudder at the memory of our first excursion with Paul, when he was living in the nursing home in Florida. Carolyn and I decided to drive him to a nature walk we had heard about. We thought he'd enjoy seeing some tropical vegetation and hearing the birds. It was my first experience in helping an invalid from a wheelchair into a car seat, and I hoped Paul wouldn't notice how nervous I was. When we arrived at our destination, I saw six steps and no ramps—and I had never negotiated a wheelchair over steps. It was a bumpy ride for Paul, but Carolyn was there to help, and the three of us learned from that experience.

Moving from Wheelchair to Car

Let's start with the maneuver of transfer. The technique is useful not only for transferring a person from wheelchair to car seat, but also from wheelchair to bed or to dining room chair, and vice versa.

The nature of the disability determines how the maneuver is carried out. Your loved one may be frail or stiff-jointed from arthritis or an operation. (After her hip fracture, Anna was in this condition.) A *paraplegic* is paralyzed from the waist down, but usually has developed strong arm muscles. A *quadriplegic* is paralyzed from the neck down and cannot use any limbs. A *hemiplegic* is paralyzed on one side of the body and cannot use the leg and arm on that side (Paul was a hemiplegic).

If your loved one still walks, even minimally, and is

able to stand, both of you can more easily effect the maneuver. Provide some support to assist him to sit comfortably. Likely you will need to help place his legs inside the car.

A hemiplegic requires more support and help. Once the person is standing and holding onto the roof of the car or the car door, move the wheelchair away so you can stand beside him. Provide underarm support and also hold onto his waist, gripping the belt or side. Help the person to turn or pivot and assist him with seating; then help him to pivot again so he faces forward. Lift his legs during this maneuver. When you exit, reverse this procedure.

A paraplegic learns to accomplish this maneuver on his own. You've doubtless seen many such disabled persons driving specially equipped cars. They remove one of the side arms of the wheelchair and grab the steering wheel or seat belt to slide themselves onto the seat. I've often been amazed to see a paraplegic go on to fold his wheelchair, lift it, and place it inside the car.

A quadriplegic is usually transported by van while still seated in a wheelchair. Otherwise, a person with this kind of disability has to be lifted up and onto another seat or bed. A strong person can do it by placing an arm under the knees and another under the shoulders, but this maneuver is more easily performed by two people. A special plastic or wooden transfer board is sometimes used to aid the sliding maneuver from wheelchair to car seat.

These various transfer maneuvers are illustrated and

described in pamphlets available through your local Heart Association office.

Don't be afraid to handle another human body. Not everyone is fragile, and you will learn as you practice the procedure. Your objective is comfort within the bounds of safety.

You'll learn where it's best for you to stand, how to brace yourself, how much support to give, where to place the wheelchair for entry or exit, when to raise the footrests of the wheelchair, and so on.

If your loved one is disoriented as well as disabled, you will have to repeat the instructions or the steps of what you are doing. Gently give instructions about when to stand, where to grab, when to pivot, and when to sit.

Check that the wheels of the wheelchair are locked, especially during transfer maneuvers. And always use the seat belt for your loved one as well as for yourself.

When making transfers in the home—from wheelchair to a chair, for example—choose a sturdy chair with arms, if possible. If you transfer a person to a straight-backed chair without arms, have a sturdy table or walker close by for additional support.

Maneuvering and Hauling the Wheelchair

It will often be necessary for you to push the wheelchair. Stairs and curbs are difficult to negotiate, as are some doors—particularly into restrooms.

When I approach a curb from the street, I push down

on the back handles of the wheelchair to lift up the front wheels; once those front wheels are on the curb (and sidewalk), I lift up and push. When returning to street level, I walk backwards, with my feet on the street and the wheelchair on the sidewalk. I push down on the wheelchair handle, pulling the patient with me and rolling the wheelchair down the curb on the big wheels. There are extensions at the bottom, which you press down with your foot to raise the front wheels.

Everyone pushes up inclines. Some folks prefer to walk backwards down an incline, bracing themselves against the weight of the wheelchair and patient.

Never attempt to go through a revolving door or walk on an escalator with a wheelchair. Find a convenient side door. Multi-story buildings all have readily accessible elevators. You may have to hunt for an elevator in a shopping mall, but there is one somewhere.

Usually you will transport the wheelchair with you. If you do this often, you'll appreciate a lighter-weight unit that allows armrests and footrests to be removed or folded for easy storage in the trunk or back seat. Exterior wheelchair carriers are available. Some are mounted on the roof of the vehicle, and the wheelchair is lifted and lowered by electrical or hydraulic power. Others are mounted on the back bumper and are similar to bicycle carriers. Secure information from your rehabilitation commission office or durable medical goods store.

Telephone ahead to see if the doctor's or dentist's office

already has a wheelchair you could borrow upon your arrival. A few department stores and shopping malls now offer this public service as well. I wish more churches did.

A Car or a Van?

What kind of vehicle is best for transporting handicapped persons?

Just about any car except the smallest compacts will do. I was surprised to discover that my mid-sized Mercury had more leg and head room than Paul's old gas-guzzling Dodge. Be sure you're buying enough leg room and a large enough trunk (or storage area, in a station wagon) for a wheelchair.

Some families decide to invest in a van. Although such vehicles sit higher off the ground than regular automobiles, the middle seats can be removed and the wider doors allow for entry of the person and wheelchair without transfer to another seat. The trick is to get the person and the wheelchair into the van.

Homemade ramps of plywood are not recommended because they are heavy and hard to handle. Commercial metal ramps are the least expensive. Some are double-track ramps that can be folded and stored for transport. These are portable, and can be used for other purposes, such as inclines over curbs or steps. Other metal ramps are full-width spring-loaded folding models that are bolted to the van floor and mounted just inside the side or rear doors. The most expensive devices are mechanical lifts. Van owners should also consider installing tie-downs and recessed "wells" in the floor. The tie-downs provide safety. The "wells" lower the wheelchair by a few inches, and provide comfort and better view for a disabled passenger.

Some recreational vehicles adapt themselves to the transportation of handicapped persons. However, most RV doors are narrow. Strategically placed grab bars and a removable ramp would help.

Public Transportation

Many metropolitan bus systems offer special transportation to handicapped persons, as do some taxi companies. The vehicles are specially adapted vans or minibuses, with raised roofs and hydraulic or electric lifts. Wheelchairs are locked to the vehicle floor. Taxi fares may have a surcharge. City bus fares will also be higher because the service provided is door-to-door, but charges will be lower than taxi fares. Hours of service may be limited so investigate what might be available in your area.

The Need for a Change of Scene

Everyone needs a change of scenery—whether it's just a drive around town, to a lake, or to a nearby shopping center. Some older people love traveling; others are reluctant to leave the security of the nursing home. Anna became more and more reluctant to leave the home. Even when we took her for short drives just to enjoy a warm, sunny day, she became increasingly nervous, and, I thought, even frightened.

Paul was delighted to travel whenever we had the time

or the inclination. We took him to church every two or three weeks. We went to cafeterias to enjoy a greater selection of food. We made several all-day excursions—to a state park, the LBJ Ranch, the San Antonio Zoo, and even took a glass-bottom boat trip! These excursions were especially fun because they often included a picnic with other family members. Our longest trip with Paul by auto was the Dallas-Fort Worth airport, some 200 miles away, where Paul took a direct flight to Orlando to spend time with his brothers.

Air Travel

Airlines are cooperative and helpful with handicapped passengers. They allow for early boarding at the gate (as well as debarking) with the airline's wheelchair, providing you ask for this service in advance. They will also check a wheelchair and walker as regular baggage. One is not required to go first class to receive these services. Most require that someone travel with the disabled person.

Always Plan Ahead

Remember, any trip—short or long—requires advance planning.

For example, barrier-free easy access and availability of adequate restroom facilities for handicapped persons are essential criteria. We had a list of eating places in Austin that provide barrier-free access, but we often telephoned ahead to ask specific questions about ramps, restroom facilities, and special parking arrangements.

There is a church we once visited with difficulty. Its only access was an entrance with three steps. The steps were high and shallow, so the only way to enter was for two people actually to lift a disabled person in his wheelchair up the stairs and into the foyer. New pews were subsequently installed, and the aisles were narrowed to accommodate more people. A wheelchair could no longer be manuevered around corners and pews which meant an older person had to leave his wheelchair in the foyer and walk, with his walker, to the nearest accessible seat. Restrooms in this church were in the basement, and could be reached from the sanctuary only by walking down a circular stairway.

One cafeteria we no longer patronize has delicious food, but it was impossible to get into the men's room with a wheelchair. One door opened into a narrow corridor, where the entrances to the men's and women's restrooms were located. Entering this second door from the narrow passageway with a wheelchair was almost impossible. The restroom itself contained no grab bars for the handicapped.

On the other hand, it was a joy to take Paul to the new Special Events Center at the University of Texas. Specially designed areas are reserved for the handicapped. There is plenty of room for wheelchairs, and folding chairs are brought in for attendants. The sight line is superb. The center has plenty of ramps, elevators, and barrier-free restrooms.

Incidentally, we've discovered that all of the newer rest

stops on interstate highways are also barrier-free. The availability of appropriate restrooms, no matter how far you travel, is of great importance and must be part of your planning.

Savor the Moments

Enjoy the adventure of traveling with your handicapped loved one. The opportunities for exciting change—for both of you—are many. The trips don't have to be long. With experience and planning, your effort will go a long way to add some adventure to your lives.

8
Personal Hygiene and Grooming

Older people sometimes give the impression that they no longer care about personal appearance. For a few, this is likely due to carelessness or listlessness. For many, however, I think it may be failing eyesight or a physical handicap that restricts personal grooming.

Cleanliness is important, both for the patient's health and for the comfort of others. Odors are caused by being bedridden, by loss of bladder and bowel control, and perhaps by a faster rate of dying cells as well as metabolic change. The only solution is frequent bathing and frequent change of clothes and bed linens.

Bathing and Showering
Nursing home staff try to change soiled clothing and bed linen with regularity. Most nursing homes have a require-

ment that staff sponge-bathe patients whenever soiling occurs. However, I discovered that Paul and Anna were showered only twice a week, and their hair wasn't always shampooed with each shower.

Nursing homes have bathtubs, often with sophisticated whirlpool attachments for massage and therapy. However, these are used only when ordered or prescribed by the attending physician.

Home care provides an opportunity for more frequent attention to personal hygiene. We encouraged a daily shower when Anna lived with us; after she moved into the retirement residence facility, we tried to include a weekly bath when she visited us. Hydraulic swivel bath chairs are helpful to lower a patient into a bathtub, as low as two inches from the bottom. Shower chairs of several types are available through durable medical goods stores. Some of the massage-type shower heads—preferably the kind with extension hoses—would add variety and perhaps relaxation to the shower.

I have often wished for the European-type of bidet, both for home care and in nursing homes. A hand-held shower head helps to shower a person who is handicapped and is seated in the bathtub (on one of the special stools available for this purpose). Installing an extra-long length of shower hose to reach the commode would serve the same purpose.

Living with Incontinence
Accept the fact that accidents will happen. One dictionary

defines *incontinence* as "inability of the body to control the evacuative functions." It isn't planned, it isn't deliberate, and it's never a reason for scolding.

Since incontinence is a major cause of bad odor, do what you can to help a patient with this problem. We provided a portable commode at our parents' bedsides. We encouraged use of the bathroom before leaving home (or the nursing home) for a visit to church, the doctor, or a restaurant. We tried to minimize night-time accidents. This is more easily accomplished with male patients, since their catheters are used externally. Talk with your doctor about catheter needs for male and female patients.

Protect furniture and beds with pads, change clothing, sponge-bathe, and use lots of powder and deodorant. It isn't easy for children to care for their parents in this very personal way, but it is a necessity with no alternative. It can be a loving service if you handle it tactfully, patiently, and professionally.

Provide your loved one with an adequate supply of underwear. You might want to consider using protective liners and pads if incontinence is constant.

Skin and Nail Care

This is not particularly a matter of personal hygiene, but a few drops of bath or baby oil on a damp washcloth rubbed onto the back, arms, and calves helps the patient feel more comfortable during colder months and combats psoriasis.

Give attention to hands and nails. Carolyn and I always

carried a pre-moistened towelette and nail clippers with a file whenever we visited Anna or Paul. Both often required hand and nail care. Since Anna ate mostly with her fingers, clean hands were a matter of health.

Hair Care

Don't overlook hair care. Hair should be shampooed with each shower. Oils build up on the scalp, and the scalp needs to be kept clean. Hair care also includes consideration of the appropriate hair style. Anna had beautiful long hair that she sometimes braided, but more often wore in a bun. As her disorientation increased, she constantly rearranged her hair. It became a frantic activity—removing and losing hairpins, tying her long hair in knots, and never really combing or brushing it.

Carolyn and I decided that cutting her hair would be best for her. Anna had never visited a beautician in her life, but this was a "parenting decision" we had to make. We didn't think she would be sufficiently patient to go through the process of getting a permanent, so we chose a short bob and arranged to have her hair cut every six or eight weeks. Now her hair was too short to knot and was easy to comb. For women less disoriented than my mother, a regular visit to the beauty shop could become a highlight of the week or month. Most nursing homes set aside a room that doubles as both beauty and barber shop, with licensed people providing services once or twice a week. Costs are much lower than in commercial shops.

Oral Hygiene

If possible, encourage your loved one to brush his teeth or soak his dentures. If your loved one isn't able to manage this task, you or the nursing staff will have to see that it's done. Dentures should be soaked each night in a cleaning agent. They should be brushed with a stronger denture cleaner periodically. Mechanical denture cleaners are available for home use. If your loved one has natural teeth, you may have to assist in brushing them.

If your loved one lives in a nursing home, provide toothpaste, denture powder or cleaning tablets, mouthwash, a denture container, powder, bath oil, shaving cream and lotion, and for men, some sort of razor (preferably electric).

Clothes Do Help Morale

Provide a sufficient change of attractive and appropriate clothing for your loved one, probably more than was used in "normal" times Buy colors she enjoys; there's no need to be drab. Appropriateness refers to the weather or climate control of the nursing home as well as to your loved one's modesty needs.

Laundry can be done at the nursing home; sometimes it's included in the overall fee. If you choose to launder your loved one's clothing yourself, plan to do this at least twice a week, as clothing must be changed often. Whether laundry is done at the nursing home or in your home, clothes will wear out faster than usual. High-strength industrial detergents are used in institutional laundries, and clothing is soiled and washed more often.

So choose *washable* clothing. Retain one or two more formal outfits for special occasions, but remember that dry cleaning is more expensive and takes longer than laundering.

One day we realized we had given away all of Anna's good dresses, since she wore only pantsuits or house dresses. We also realized that we no longer had a burial dress for her. Setting aside a favorite dress or suit for those last rites isn't morbid—it's practical. As your loved one's level of disability increases, you will tend to purchase clothing of a more "leisure" nature, although you may want to retain some more "formal" wear for special occasions. Pantsuits with a minimum of buttons, fasteners, or zippers are the most practical items for women. You may want to experiment with Velcro fasteners. Long, warm housecoats and washable sweaters are also useful.

Sport shirts and doubleknit, washable slacks are practical for men. If your loved one was a dapper dresser, provide a few dress shirts and clip-on ties he might be able to put on by himself. He'll also enjoy a sweater or two.

For additional warmth, consider shawls or ponchos. Lap robes are useful but should be machine washable.

Include purchases of clothing in your family budget. It is also your responsibility to see that clothing is kept in good repair.

Label Personal Items
If your loved one lives in a nursing home, all clothing, in-

cluding socks and stockings, should be marked or labeled with indelible ink pens or iron-on fabric tape. Make a point of checking clothing on a regular basis. Marking ink isn't really "permanent"; names wash out and tags come off. Each nursing home has a place where stacks of unidentified clothing are stored; check through these from time to time to retrieve what is your loved one's and then label it again. It's also a good idea to label eyeglasses and even dentures. Both have a way of getting misplaced in a nursing home, and it's hard to identify your loved one's from everyone else's! Use pressure-sensitive letter-tape for glasses, or lightly etch your loved one's initials on them. Etch initials lightly on dentures or place some kind of identifying mark on them.

Be a Valet

Since clothing tends to get mixed up in nursing homes, it's a good idea to rearrange clothing in your loved one's closet. Not every aide is color-conscious or takes the time to think in terms of clothing ensembles. Putting the right shirt with the right pair of slacks on the same hanger (or the appropriate blouse with the right slacks or skirt) will help. You're blessed if you have an aide who enjoys dressing your loved one in something clean, fresh, and color-coordinated *every* day.

Shoes and Slippers

Footwear requires special attention, too.

For most patients warm, washable slippers or slipper-socks are practical. Since these get soiled and wet, several changes are recommended. I found that open-toe, all plastic shoes with buckles were practical for Anna. These could be washed, rinsed, and dried by hand. Knee-length socks are also appropriate, for both men and women. Check heels and soles for needed repairs. Apply wax and polish when needed since this isn't normally done by anyone in nursing homes.

If your loved one requires a foot brace, your orthopedist or physiatrist will prescribe the right type and weight of brace. These may be attached to a sturdy, serviceable older pair of shoes. However, not every shoe repair shop is willing or able to do this kind of specialized work. Telephone in advance to learn where this kind of work can be done.

Feeling good about yourself is often a matter of grooming and dress. Encourage these good feelings in your loved ones by attending to these details.

An Important Reminder
The following soliloquy was found in the belongings of a woman who died in the geriatric ward of a hospital near Dundee, Scotland.

Nurses at the hospital were so impressed with the poem that they copied it and had it distributed to every nurse in the hospital. The poem was taken to Ireland, where it was copied again. An American missionary nurse saw it in New Zealand and brought it to the United States.

We don't know the name of the woman who wrote it.

However, as you ponder the implications of this chapter—which are really concerned with personal dignity and self-esteem—this view of an older person by a perceptive and talented "oldster" can speak to each one of us.

A Crabbit Old Woman Wrote This

What do you see, nurses, what do you see?
Are you thinking when you are looking at me—
A crabbit old woman, not very wise,
Uncertain of habit, with faraway eye,
Who dribbles her food and makes no reply
When you say in a loud voice—"I do wish you'd try."
Who seems not to notice the things that you do,
And forever is losing a stocking or shoe.
Who, unresisting or not, lets you do as you will,
With bathing and feeding, the long day to fill.
Is that what you're thinking? Is that what you see?
Then open your eyes, nurse, you're looking at me.
I tell you who I am as I sit here so still;
As I use at your bidding, as I eat at your will,
I'm a small child often with a father and mother,
Brothers and sisters, who love one another.
A young girl of sixteen, with wings on her feet.
Dreaming that soon now a lover she'll meet;
A bride soon a-twenty, my heart gives a leap,
Remembering the vows that I promised to keep;
At twenty-five now I have young of my own,
Who need me to build a secure, happy home;

A woman of thirty, my young now grow fast,
Bound to each other with ties that should last.
At forty, my young sons have grown and gone,
But my man's beside me to see I don't mourn.
At fifty, once more babies play round my knee,
Again we know children, my loved one and me.
Dark days are upon me, my husband is dead,
I look to the future, I shudder with dread.
For my young are all rearing young of their own,
And I think of the years and the love that I've known.
I'm now an old woman and nature is cruel—
'Tis jest to make old age look like a fool.
The body it crumbles, grace and vigor depart,
There now is a stone where I once had a heart.
But inside this old carcass a young girl still dwells,
And now again my battered heart swells.
I remember the joys, I remember the pain.
And I'm loving and living life over again.
I think of the years all too few gone too fast,
And accept the stark fact that nothing can last.
So open your eyes, nurse, open and see
NOT a crabbit old woman, LOOK closer,
SEE ME!

9
Some Tips on Nutrition

Most books on diet or health foods affirm in some way that "you are what you eat." *Live Longer and Better* is such a book, written by physician Robert Clifford Peale, brother of Norman Vincent. The right kinds of food are especially important for people as they grow older.

Essential Nutrition
Professional nutritionists no longer agree on which "basic foods" are, in fact, essential. However, there is widespread agreement that all of us still need to include in our *daily* diet green and yellow vegetables, fruit, milk or milk products, protein, bread and cereals, and some fat in the form of butter or fortified margarine.

The vegetables can be cooked (frozen or canned, but preferably fresh and *steamed* to retain nutritional value) or eaten raw.

Raw cabbage or salad greens are substitutes for citrus fruits.

Milk can be fluid or in the form of cheese or custards.

Protein is available not only in red meat but also in poultry, fish, eggs, beans, peas, nuts, and peanut butter. Rice and beans—a South American staple—is a remarkably good source of complete protein (containing all the essential amino acids). Soy products are also high in protein.

Protein builds and repairs body tissues. Protein deficiency in infants produces *kwashiorkor,* a disease prevalent in the hunger areas of our world. One of the serious effects of *kwashiorkor* is brain damage. Evidence is mounting that protein deficiency also has a serious effect on the brains of older people, and that a balanced diet that includes protein can have some restorative effect.

Our chief sources of calories (from which our bodies derive heat and energy) are carbohydrates and fats. Fats provide more than twice as many calories per gram as carbohydrates. For example, one tablespoon of butter has as many calories (100) as two tablespoons of sugar. Potatoes, bread, beans, and rice are all good sources of carbohydrates.

Vitamins and Minerals
All of us require a balanced diet with the proper mix of vitamins and minerals.

Vitamin A helps maintain health of mucous membranes and skin.

The B vitamins are necessary for our nervous systems, for healthy skin and hair, for good digestion, and to help us better utilize carbohydrates and fats. Niacin deficiency is thought to result in a poor mental state and poor skin condition.

Vitamin C is essential for normal body growth, but older people need it for upkeep of bones and teeth. Many people believe this vitamin helps prevent colds.

Vitamin D also promotes growth and assists in absorption of phosphorus and calcium for bones and teeth. Except for those who cannot tolerate milk, the dairy industry's slogan is correct: "You never outgrow your need for milk."

Iron builds blood, while iodine helps the thyroid. Minerals lost in commercial food processing must be replaced.

Irregularity and Nutrition

According to advertisers, most elderly persons suffer from some kind of constipation or irregularity.

The medical advice I've received from our doctors is not to become overly anxious if an older patient doesn't have a daily bowel movement. In fact, don't worry if bowel movements aren't any more frequent than every three days, as long as your loved one is eating a well-balanced diet, with raw fruits and vegetables. Include bran and that old standby, prunes or prune juice. Some people find that a daily glass of buttermilk is helpful. Adequate exercise is also beneficial for proper elimination.

If a laxative is necessary, ask your doctor about one of the milder "bulk" preparations such as *Effersyllium* or *Metamucil*.

Overnutrition and Undernutrition

As parents of growing children, we learned to prepare foods and monitor eating habits so that essential dietary and nutritional requirements were met. Younger children are often enticed to eat sweet cereals or snacks. Many teenagers are undernourished due to their diet of French fries, hamburgers, pizza, and soft drinks.

Our aging loved ones may not exercise their best judgment where eating is concerned. They may rely too much upon breakfast cereal or an occasional TV dinner if they live at home. Preparing their own food may seem to be "too much bother." Institutional food may be unpalatable and unchewable.

Some Questions for Dieticians

Institutional meals have been widely criticized. There is blandness, overcooking, and little use of natural foods.

I am often distressed that institutions providing health care seem to be so little concerned with the food that is cooked and served to patients. I know that many good, qualified people serve as nutritionists and staff dieticians, but the nutritional and culinary state-of-the-art in hospitals and nursing homes in far behind CAT scans, intercoms, labs, or intensive-care units.

I'm distressed enough to want to ask a few questions

(which may also apply to home cooking):

Why is so much white bread served? Older people can enjoy eating whole wheat bread (preferably stone ground), which provides more nutrients and fiber. Why couldn't institutions bake their own bread, rolls, and muffins on the premises? The smell of baking would be an improvement over some other odors in nursing homes.

Why not provide healthy snack foods like fruit and vegetables? Apples might be difficult for some to eat, but most elderly people can manage other fruits. Most have no difficulty with carrot sticks, stalks of celery, or pieces of raw cauliflower and zucchini squash. Fruits and vegetables cut down on the desire for sugar, a good thing for older people with their increased risk of developing diabetes.

Fruit juice and fruit punch would satisfy the craving for something sweet, provide some vitamins, and enhance kidney function. And fruit juice would be much better than a pot of coffee.

While I am mentioning snacks, I propose that vending machines be banned from patient quarters and areas. Sick and convalescing people do not need junk food and soft drinks. Perhaps the machines could be modified to sell nuts, raisins, or dried bananas. If vending machines must be kept, keep them in staff lounges.

Couldn't cottage cheese and yogurt be used more? How about hot cereals for breakfast—and grains such as millet and barley and brown rice for other meals, instead of the usual dehydrated potatoes?

There are nutritional advantages in steam-cooking vegetables. But Chinese-type cooking is beneficial in other ways. Stir-frying "extends" meat, doesn't cook vegetables to death, and smaller pieces of food are easier to eat.

Meat doesn't always have to be served as chopped hamburger. Perhaps broiled turbot or some other inexpensive fish might be served. The price of chicken is always reasonable, and there are many ways to serve it besides fried. Meat substitutes such as soy products can be used alone in casseroles or as meat extenders.

Ban deep-frying! It doesn't help digestion or cholesterol count.

Liver is a good source of iron and vitamin A, although high in cholesterol. Must it always be served in fried, leathery form? Most people don't like liver, so it has to be made tasty. There are recipes to disguise liver in new ways.

Why aren't more casseroles prepared in hospitals and nursing homes? This is a great way to combine dietary essentials in a flavorful, convenient form.

Why not substitute honey for sugar? White sugar is a highly processed food with no nutritive value. Brown sugar is better, if it isn't artificially colored. Honey contains a few minerals and is a potent sweetener.

The Value of Good Nutrition

Some of these ideas appear costly. Honey is more expensive than white sugar, and perhaps more staff time would be needed for baking, preparing carrot sticks, or making casseroles. It might require more fuel to cook buckwheat than to make mashed potatoes from a dehydrated mix.

But would it matter if food and food preparation did cost a bit more? *Food is part of health care!* The daily charges in hospitals and nursing homes are shockingly high. Perhaps the time has come to insist that a greater percentage of our health-care dollar go into the right kind of food, properly prepared.

New cooking techniques would have to be learned, but most kitchen staffs would welcome the opportunity to learn and to be innovative, particularly when they understand the reasons behind better nutrition in the meals they prepare. Food processors, industrial mixers, steamers, and ovens aren't that expensive, and they cut down on food preparation time. Much could be done with the equipment already in hand.

Food *Can* Be Appetizing

There are a few elderly people who never seem satisfied with the food they are served—or simply do not have much of an appetite. Some of this is due to the loss of tastebuds. Making food colorful and using condiments may help whet jaded or frustrated appetites. I have seen excellent and attractive meals served in nursing homes. But I have also witnessed strange, colorless combinations of purees that turned my stomach.

Older people who can no longer use a fork or spoon

still need balanced meals that can be eaten by hand with a minimum of messiness—for example, small chunks of meat without sauce or gravy, some small boiled potatoes or beets, cooked carrots, and some apple slices. Meals don't have to be tasteless, textureless, and colorless.

The Danger of Leftovers

People who live alone often do not eat properly. They tend to snack and don't bother to cook food, or they rely on prepackaged foods. Anna subsisted for too many years on hot tea and raisin bread.

Dr. Jurgen Schmandt, a political scientist/nutritionist at the University of Texas, believes that older people should never keep leftovers. Too often leftovers become the basis for the next meal or even the next several meals. They are eaten cold and do not provide a balanced meal.

Check on the meal habits of loved ones who live independently. Check their refrigerators from time to time, just to make sure there are no leftovers or other items waiting to spoil or to become the inadequate makings of future meals. You could provide your own version of balanced "TV dinners" in single portions that are frozen and can be reheated easily. Make sure your loved one has cans of soup, breakfast cereal, and healthy snacks such as nuts or raisins or dried fruit.

If you don't live close to your loved one, make arrangements with a friend who can check for you or enroll your loved one in either a delivered-meal ("meals-on-wheels") or a congregate-meal ("meals-on-heels") program.

Hints for Jaded Appetites

Each of us has experienced days when even the thought of food wasn't appealing. There are many such days for the elderly, but there are also many nutritious ways to reactivate their appetites.

Our 1946 edition of Irma Rombauer's classic *The Joy of Cooking* included a small section titled "Invalid or Convalescent Cookery."

Here are a few tasty, easy-to-chew items from her list to appeal to tired appetites.

There are dozens of soups: broths, boullions, cream soups, minestrone, borscht (beet soup), and Swedish fruit soups.

Soufflés can be prepared with strained vegetables, chicken, mushrooms, or cheese. Custards, puddings, omelets, and flavored gelatin are quite pleasing.

How about stews that can be eaten with a spoon: chicken (perhaps with dumplings), oyster, beef, or lamb? Meat pies offer more possibilities. *The Joy of Cooking* includes a recipe for a cornmeal mush meat pie; creamed chicken could be substituted for the meat. This is similar to the various kinds of shepherds' pies.

Better Food for Public Places by Anne Moyer emphasizes nutrition and natural foods. Recipes for six "complete protein meatless casseroles" are given. It also offers recipes for ham and bean soup, beef barley soup, cabbage soup, corn chicken soup, lentil soup, and potato soup. Some suggested salads are egg, tuna, ham, curried chicken, or pineapple chicken—all of which include raw vegetables and nuts. More use can be made of sprouts and tofu (soybean curd). Meat loaf can be prepared with oatmeal. Tomatoes can be broiled. There's a good recipe for eggplant parmesan and much more.

There are many possibilities for serving nutritious, tasty, and economical food. A bit of imagination, planning, and preparation is required. Surely the benefits are worth the extra effort.

10
Handy Hints
on Exercise

One of the sad byproducts of our sedentary existence is loss of muscle tone and, thus, loss of energy. Those of us who are desk-bound know the feeling and can more easily recognize what is happening to our handicapped loved ones. For them lack of exercise often results in atrophying limbs and muscles.

Exercise is essential for all of us. Although the bedridden are limited by what they can do, they can benefit from some simple exercises.

Walking

For most seniors, walking is still one of the best ways to keep fit. Physical therapy can help achieve a measure of mobility. Some may require assistance (Paul needed a steady grip on his belt and shoulder to aid his sense of balance). Or a walker may be used to give additional stability. Don't overprotect, but practice safety first. Be available if you are needed to keep an older person from falling.

There are many places for pleasant walks, indoors and outdoors. We walked with Paul almost every time we visited him at the Trinity Home. Try long wide hallways if it's snowing or raining, or a short jaunt around the block in the sunshine. If you don't find places to walk, rent or purchase some sort of inexpensive treadmill with sturdy side rails and set it up in a bedroom, a den, or in the garage.

Establish a routine of walking; keeping to it will assist digestion and elimination and get the blood flowing back toward the heart. For the elderly, walking is usually better and safer than jogging.

If your loved one receives physical therapy, ask the therapist to teach you the rudiments of "gait assistance"— walking with a handicapped person. Practice with the therapist's supervision. You'll develop a new skill. Although walking will be more slowly paced, it will give you time to chat and observe things as you walk. The time spent walking with a loved one can become the best part of a visit.

Cycling
Cycling is one way many older people can get exercise.

Of course, it's more practical for those who cycled in their youth and have continued the habit. Bicycle together, selecting routes that are reasonably level and safe.

An exercycle might be an option. Adapter accessories can convert an ordinary bicycle into a stationary, safe exercycle without the expense of having to buy the real thing.

Large adult-sized tricycles ("tri-wheelers") are coming into vogue and are common in many retirement villages. Anyone with the use of arms and legs can ride one, since balance isn't required. Depending upon the amount of traffic, they are reasonably safe (they should not be used in busy thoroughfares). Large wire baskets provide a place where groceries or plants or packages may be transported. These adult tricycles cost between three and five hundred dollars and are a practical substitute for automobiles in a neighborhood setting.

Other Sports

Jogging and tennis are strenuous and exhausting sports and should be initiated or continued only with medical approval. Golf might be a better choice.

Swimming is good exercise and has therapeutic value. Special classes that teach the handicapped to swim—or teach new techniques of swimming—are available in many larger cities. Consult city recreation departments or your local Heart Association for information. Because specially designed facilities and individual instruction are required, costs are sometimes high.

At fifty-eight, Dr. James Counsilman, swimming coach at Indiana University, swam the English Channel. He is the oldest person to have accomplished this feat. Dr. Counsilman is a professional swimmer, has coached several Olympic gold medalists, and proves that with vigorous participation a sport can be continued into more mature years to the point of great endurance.

But one does not have to aim at changing the record books.

For most of us swimming is simply a healthy way to relax and strengthen muscles, including the heart, and to relieve the discomfort of back ailments and swollen joints.

Golf involves many muscles through walking, bending, pulling, and swinging. It provides the additional benefits of fresh air and sun.

Most team sports are too physically demanding for older persons. However, those who were active in softball, basketball, or volleyball might manage some continuing but more restricted involvement.

Some of us have too quickly dismissed *horseshoes* and *shuffleboard* with a condescending smile, seeing them as images of insipid retirement. But both provide healthy exercise with socialization, fun, and fresh air.

Badminton, croquet, and *ping-pong (table tennis)* are other physical activities to consider.

The point is this: As long as we are able, it is important that we exercise muscles and stimulate the circulation of blood in whatever ways are appropriate and possible, so we don't become bedridden and allow our muscles to atrophy. Even as we grow older, we can maintain healthy bodies and a high energy level with a will-to-do-it. Exercise helps to relieve tension and enhances the way we feel about ourselves.

Group Exercise

Dr. Garland O'Quinn, formerly a professor of physical education at the University of Texas in Austin and an Olympic medalist in gymnastics, is now a leader and consultant in developing exercise programs for handicapped persons of all ages. He emphasizes that the purpose of exercise for older people is to encourage people to feel good about themselves and to be happy. Thus, Dr. O'Quinn is cautious about prescribing a rigid physical activity plan for anyone.

However, he cites at least three benefits that result from limited and somewhat structured group exercise.

1. *Music usually accompanies group exercise.* Hearing and reacting to music is in itself beneficial, says O'Quinn. The rhythm helps pace the group and there is less physical strain. Children's activities records are sometimes adaptable for this purpose. One is called *Get Fit While You Sit* (released by Educational Activities, Inc., and available through most record stores). O'Quinn has a record called *Light 'n Lively* (a Melody House release).

2. *People can learn to maintain and enjoy the physical abilities they still have.* Group exercise for older citizens is not intended to train persons for the Olympics but to increase a healthy awareness and respect for one's body.

3. *Group exercise, no matter how minimal, will get the blood moving.* The heart pumps blood to our extremities, but the job of helping the heart to pump it back belongs to our muscles. Another physiological benefit of exercise is that more oxygen will get to the lungs. The body will be healthier because of exercise.

When you have an opportunity to encourage and lead exercise programs in rest homes or nursing homes, Dr. O'Quinn cautions not to insist upon total participation. You're not running a military physical fitness program; participation should be an individual decision. People will vary from day to day in their desire to participate and share. They may not feel well, or a gloomy day may induce a gloomy spirit. Observing others can be a mood-lifter, along with tapping toes or fingers to the music or sharing in the laughter.

Here are some exercises that older people can do:

Stand-ups. Rising from a chair to a standing position and sitting down again is a helpful exercise (and sometimes notable achievement) for many older people. This activity can be enhanced by making it a rhythmic routine. For persons with leg disabilities or loss of balance, it's helpful to have chairs with armrests so the person has something to push up against. They also ought to have a companion close by to give assistance, if needed.

Resistance exercise. A partner is needed for this isometric exercise. Both partners either stand or sit facing each other. One person makes fists with both hands, while the partner encloses these with open hands. One pushes outward with his fists while the other pushes inward with his open palms for no more than three or four seconds. (Dr. O'Quinn cautions that it is very important not to carry this exercise to the point of strain.) Or one person can push downward while the other pushes upward. Partners exchange "roles" and direction of pressure. The procedure is to count to four and alternate.

Moving arms and shoulders. You can establish a simple routine of rhythmic calisthenics, whether seated or standing. (1) Extend your arms in front of you; (2) place at your sides; (3) to your knees; (4) at your sides; (5) extend arms above you; (6) again at your sides; (7) twist torso to left, moving arms; (8) then twist torso to the right, moving arms. Count to eight as you demonstrate this exercise. Repeat four or five times. This is a simple exercise, but it gets the circulation going.

Moving legs and feet. This exercise should be done while seated. Establish a rhythmic count. Extend both legs. Raise the right leg and put it down. Raise the left leg and put it down. Raise both legs and put them down (this is hard to do; participants may need to push down on the seats of their chairs to do this part). This exercise can be done to the count of twelve with two counts to each movement.

Here's another way to exercise legs and feet. With the legs extended, turn or twist feet so the toes touch, then turn or twist feet so the heels touch. Repeat a dozen times to music.

Reminiscence exercise. This works well with chairbound

111

persons. Talk about washing clothes in "the old days." Encourage the person to talk and to follow your motions. Rub the clothes up and down an imaginary washboard. Wring a wet towel slowly and carefully with wrist motions. Raise hands to pin the washing to clothes lines. Iron a shirt. Fold towels. Muscle toning and improved circulation may be the result, along with some good conversation. (Try chopping wood, pumping water, rowing, milking, and so on.)

Body Movements

There are many simple warm-up exercises that are good preparation for more serious exercise. It's recommended that music be used in warming up as well as in regular exercising. Perhaps you can encourage other residents to join you and your loved one in these movements.

Even seriously disoriented people enjoy clapping. Begin by counting to the rhythm, then switch to clapping hands and then hitting knees. Or even try flapping elbows up and down in cadence!

An alternative to clapping is to hit the palm of the left hand eight times with the fist of the right hand; then reverse the activity.

If you're playing a march, let the people march. If they have difficulty walking, they can "march" where they are seated by raising one foot and then the other. Or have them wiggle their toes or touch toes and heels with each foot, all in cadence.

Try some "dancing"—which for our purposes here is

merely a euphemism for structured warm-up exercises. Contemporary dancing isn't all that complicated, and if your participants can walk, they'll manage a few simple steps. You can create a "disco" by having them take four steps forward and four steps back, twisting hips and swinging arms at will.

A similar program to Garland O'Quinn's is a physical fitness program called *Preventicare,* developed in West Virginia by Lawrence J. Frankel, a physical therapist.

He believes that exercises not only prevent poor circulation but can help aching joints and muscles, arthritis, and improve coordination and lessen chronic fatigue.

There are fifty *Preventicare* exercises that can be performed in any position a person finds most comfortable—sitting (even in a wheelchair), standing, or lying on the floor or in bed. Once learned, the exercises can be done by individuals or by groups without a "professional" on hand to supervise. Mr. Frankel concurs with Dr. O'Quinn in recommending the use of music to establish the pace. He believes the pulse of an older person should not be faster than 120 beats per minute, and music helps control the pulse rate.

Here is a sampling of his exercises:

Tilt your head backward as far as possible, and then forward as far as possible. Do this ten times.
Spread or stretch your fingers on both hands and bring them together repeatedly.
Crumple a page of a newspaper into a ball, using the

first point of each finger, not the palm. Use one hand at a time.

With both hands, push a piece of broomstick (or a large dowel) away from you, then pull it back to your chest.

Stretch out your legs and cross them, right leg over left, then left over right.

Most of these exercises conclude with the instruction, "Continue as long as you can"—good advice for all of us.

11
Making Activities Meaningful

How do we fill the hours and days of loved ones who are no longer able to live independently? This becomes an important consideration for us "caregivers."

Carolyn and I have always rebelled against any form of "busy work" for ourselves, our children, and our loved ones. But our loved ones needed ways to occupy their minds as well as their time. We wanted these to be *creative,* but we eventually recognized that there was a place for wholesome "busy work."

In this chapter I'm merely going to review some of the things we discovered. Not all of the ideas are original or novel, nor will all of these work with equal success for you, but I hope they give you a starting place.

Books

Be grateful if your loved one still enjoys reading. Books have always been a creative way to deal with isolation and depression, as well as curiosity.

Get to know the people who staff your local library. Carolyn is a librarian, so Paul and Anna had a personal librarian looking for books to challenge them. Libraries not only lend books, but also records and tapes and even large framed prints.

Libraries have books of all categories printed in large type, which may be easier for your loved one to read. *Reader's Digest* and *The New York Times Magazine* have large-print editions. *Reader's Digest* also publishes a quarterly book in large print, containing one book condensation and several articles. Check your local bookstore for a section of large-print books.

Many older people enjoy large picture books dealing with travel or nature. If they've done much traveling during their lifetime, they may enjoy remembering those places by perusing a good atlas. *National Geographic* is always interesting to look at, no matter how ancient the issue.

Identify the books in your loved one's personal library that were favorites. If the type is too small for your loved one to read, read it aloud or give this opportunity to your children or a visitor. Perhaps your loved one would like to have a favorite volume around just to touch and leaf through.

Recordings
When your loved one's eyes fail or simply can't make out the words because of brain damage, having someone read

to him is a way for him to keep up with life and ideas.

You will want to do some of this yourself. You may want to record some of this reading so your loved one could listen while you are occupied elsewhere.

However, remember that there are many services ready for your call. In many areas, National Public Radio broadcasts "From the Bookshelf" five days a week, an excellent way to "read" current bestsellers. Most bookstores sell cassette editions of popular books.

State libraries have large sections devoted to materials for the blind and visually handicapped. Books have been recorded on cassette tapes, and the federal government provides free postage to and from the library. The Library of Congress provides a free cassette player to play these tapes. Check with your state commission for the blind or your library for more information. Medical certification of need may be requested.

The Jewish Guild for the Blind specializes in recording current bestsellers, both fiction and nonfiction. Professional narrators read the books, and sound effects are sometimes incorporated to make the book come "alive."

Various Christian organizations provide devotional and Bible study materials on cassette. Some are loaned; others must be purchased. Several versions of the Scriptures have been recorded. I enjoy the version distributed by the American Bible Society, narrated by Alexander Scourby. The Reigner Library of Union Theological Seminary (Richmond, Virginia) has the most extensive listing of lectures.

If your loved one enjoys music, records can be borrowed from your library or from friends. Portable record players are often loaned as well. You might want to have favorite music recorded on cassette, as cassette players are simpler for handicapped persons to use.

Volunteer Work

As long as your loved one is able and willing, collaborate with agencies seeking volunteer help. The wisdom and expertise of elderly people is a vast, untapped resource in many fields.

Foster grandparents are needed in homes for the mentally retarded. Sitters are welcomed in daycare centers and church nurseries (churches sometimes pay a nominal stipend for this service). Volunteers are needed in nursing homes to write and read letters, to help patients with shopping, or just to be a friend to someone who doesn't have one.

Coordination of such volunteer opportunities is often done by RSVP—the *Retired Senior Volunteer Program,* funded through ACTION—usually listed in the telephone directory.

SCORE—*Service Corps of Retired Executives*—is an organization that provides free management counseling to small businessmen and community groups. For information, consult your local office of the Small Business Association.

Many cities have an Adult Services Council that provides information on services and opportunities for older adults. Check the telephone book, your local library, your local chapter of the AARP (American Association of Retired Persons), or your local welfare or human resources agency.

Crafts

A loved one who likes to sew, crochet, embroider, or knit will likely want to continue. Anna enjoyed embroidery for several years. There were two quilting groups in Paul's nursing home; one was for the "perfectionists" and the other was for those who were interested but whose attention to detail was waning.

Make sure projects are manageable. This may mean finding smaller pieces to embroider with simpler designs or providing a larger set of needles for making a larger-than-normal afghan. Your loved one might like to learn new skills in needlepoint, ceramics, or leatherworking. Materials and techniques are constantly invented; visit a craft shop every few months just to browse and get ideas.

If your loved one enjoys woodworking and is still able to use tools, this may be the opportunity to make a dollhouse for a granddaughter or a rocking horse for a great-grandson. If he is into electronics, this might be the time to get into ham radio or make a mini-computer.

Using one's skills in crafts is a fine way to make gifts for the family or to earn some extra money.

We are fortunate to have a parks and recreation department in Austin that gives serious attention to the needs of senior citizens. It operates several day activity centers.

It also provides an opportunity for displaying and selling crafts in an annual fair at the Municipal Auditorium and in a store that is open throughout the year and located on "Main Street" in Austin. Many skills are being preserved, and many people are productively happy.

Hobbies

It's difficult to begin a hobby late in life, but it is possible. Perhaps your loved one had some interest for which he or she never felt there was time; now there is time to explore, learn, and enjoy.

Many older people discover enjoyment in painting. Anna Mary Robertson Moses, better known as "Grandma Moses," began her career in her seventies.

Paul came to enjoy coloring pictures. We first supplied him with paint-by-number books that required watercolors. It was a challenge to keep the brush within the lines with his left hand, but he improved. We found posters that he colored with felt pens, and he completed these as gifts for his grandchildren. We found pictures on which pigment was already printed; they only required a wet brush. But the colors were not vivid and the pictures not much of a challenge for him. Then Carolyn found a collection of birds to color. Paul relished these and was extremely proud of his work. Carolyn placed some Audubon prints around his room to inspire him.

Dover Publications publishes a variety of coloring books, many of which deal with history, art, nostalgia, and nature. Concordia publishes oversized coloring posters. Art can be therapeutic.

Shop art supply stores just as you would craft and hobby shops. Look for new ways for handicapped persons to use color. There are many varieties of colored pencils, charcoal, and chalk. There are chalk-type materials that can be rubbed onto a picture and then painted with a wet brush. There are watercolor "brush" markers. Your loved one's dexterity, muscle coordination, ability to grip and grasp, and eyesight will determine what kinds of materials are most suitable.

Collecting stamps and coins may require a magnifying glass, but these hobbies appreciate in value and interest. Borrow the latest stamp and coin catalogs from your library. Additions to the collection make good gifts.

Perhaps your loved one collected stones but never had time to polish them. Now is the time to obtain a tumbler. This won't require much physical exertion, but the process will be fascinating. A spin-off might be some jewelry-making.

Back to Nature

Gardening and bird-watching are hobbies many older people enjoy.

We purchased a canary for Anna. She enjoyed his singing and followed the book in caring for her "Georgie."

For one of Paul's birthdays, we gave him a bird bath and feeder and placed it just outside his nursing home window. We kept both supplied weekly with seed and water. Paul delighted in the antics of his feathered friends. There were the usual sparrows, but mockingbirds, cardinals, and blue jays also visited. The birds brought enjoyment to other residents as well.

When Paul lived with us, we encouraged his interest in plants by giving him a "garden plot"—a six-foot-long window box placed on a shelf so it was within his reach. He planted lettuce and radishes in summer. Later in the year he planted flowers. He enjoyed watching the growth and participating in the harvest. This was the only part of our garden that received a superabundance of water since Paul insisted on watering his garden every day!

Later, one of Paul's friends sent him an amarlyllis plant. It arrived early enough to bloom at Easter, and it continued to bring enjoyment every spring. Plants require care, but they make fine gifts.

Games

Games are important as ways to retain mental agility and to bring people of all ages together, especially on a one-to-one basis. They help us to bridge generation gaps and to enjoy each other's company when conversation wanes or wanders.

Anna was the game player in our family. She enjoyed checkers, picture and crossword puzzles, *Monopoly,* and *Scrabble*. She used to whiz through a thousand-piece jigsaw puzzle in a day or two. Sadly, those days ended long before her death.

Paul and Anna both grew up in an environment in which

"worldliness" meant playing cards, attending movies, dancing, smoking, and drinking alcoholic beverages. The Sabbath was to be strictly observed as a day of worship and rest. Since so many sports events took place on Sundays, professional sports were ignored and certainly not encouraged. This heritage carries over to many oldsters. I'm sure Paul was often distressed with Carolyn and me for taking him to day activities centers where people actually seemed to enjoy their card games.

But Paul did become interested in sports on television. And occasionally he would tackle a picture puzzle, although it had to be simple and broad in design with large, easy-to-fit pieces. He learned to play dominoes.

Chess is another good game for older people. On my way to visit Paul at Trinity Home, I often drove past a group of four elderly men seated around a barrel in "downtown" Round Rock. They played dominoes, chess, and checkers, and I understand they usually defeated any young challenger. However, I can't remember ever seeing anyone playing chess in a nursing home, although I have seen some bridge played. If some people remember the rules of bridge, surely others remember the gambits of chess. I believe chess, backgammon, and many of the new strategy games would appeal to many older persons.

Flash cards used for phonics and word association with young children may also be excellent conversation-starters. I tried this once with Anna. She tried to speak some of the words and identified several numbers. We played with the pictures she especially liked—the sheep, the dog, the little girl with a basket of flowers. I'd put these face down on the table and she would slowly turn them over, smile, and sometimes try to speak the word.

How about the *Ungame* for its intergenerational, non-competitive fun? Or *Scrabble* (now available in Large Type and Braille editions)? There are *Chinese Checkers* with pegs. Ask about conventional checkers with unconventional square pieces as well as round ones, so visually-handicapped persons may play.

Games are a way to enliven and enrich your visits. When you find a game that really "clicks," you might want to leave it at the nursing home for your loved one and a friend to enjoy.

Some nursing homes make a special effort to encourage socialization of residents through games and parties. Bingo (without money winners) is a favorite. Monthly birthday parties are common—all residents who have had a birthday during the month are honored, and all residents are invited. Family help and participation is welcomed. Anna's nursing home began a "happy hour" twice a week from 3:00 to 4:00 P.M., when fruit punch and sandwiches or cookies were served and records played. One nursing home in the hill country of Texas has a monthly wine and cheese party.

Television
I used to think of television as a kind of sedative or an electronic "sitter" for older people.

But I'm changing my mind. One must still be selective;

some is fluff, some is destructive—shows where young and old are victimized. But we should not damn the medium just because of its product or the character of those who merchandise filth. There are good programs on TV, both on educational and commercial networks and on cable.

Anna was an avid fan until her interest span became too brief to enjoy television. Paul long enjoyed the news programs and features on TV, even before his stroke. Television was a window to his world.

I used to check the weekly TV schedule and make a chart showing the programs I thought Paul would enjoy. On a large sheet of paper, using big letters and numbers, I color-coded the time and circled the channel. I taped this chart to the wall next to his TV set. When there was a program we missed or something special like a presidential news conference, we called the nurse on duty and asked her to tell Paul and turn on the set or change channels.

Videocassette recorders allow you to record late-evening specials or a few classic motion pictures that older people never see because they are usually in bed by nine.

Radio

The homebound have enjoyed listening to the radio since its earliest days in the 1920s. We called them "shut-ins" then. Despite the abundance of television programming, especially with the new cable systems, radio may still be the preferred medium for your loved one.

Radio continues to provide news and coverage of special events and sports. FM radio brings music of all types with minimum interruption. Many radio stations target their programming to smaller audiences. There are twenty-four-hour-a-day news stations, classical music stations, ethnic stations, and Christian stations.

Radio drama is making a comeback. Mystery and adventure have returned to commercial radio. Public radio is dramatizing the classics or experimenting with new dramatic works.

Public radio presents many interesting choices. British and Canadian programs are rebroadcast. Books are read. Special coverage is given to congressional hearings.

Many listeners enjoy "talk shows"—interviews and phone-in questions and responses. Elderly persons are regular participants in such programs.

Shortwave reception is better than ever—and there is excitement in listening to Hilversum or Moscow or London or Quito.

There are even special radio sets that provide twenty-four-hour weather forecasts. You can push a button and hear your local U.S. Weather Bureau.

Radio may be an ideal companion for your loved one.

Creative Achievements

In looking through a book called *Play Activities for the Retarded Child* (by Bernice Wells Carlson and David R. Ginglend, published by Abingdon), I found ideas that might be adapted for people suffering from the classic symptoms of senility, who do not participate in the kinds of games and activities we've been discussing.

The book offers suggestions for games, crafts, and music. Many of the motion songs would be enjoyed by nursing home residents.

The authors make two points in their discussion of handicraft skills and retarded children that apply to our topic in this chapter.

First, they say it is important for a child to see *the results of his efforts*. This is especially important to a person who is constantly frustrated. Crafts, games, or activities must be simple and manageable enough so that older people can see a visible, achievable result. We must not expect too much. On the other hand, we must not do too much for them. But we can certainly try to provide creative opportunities to overcome frustration and depression.

Second, the authors point to *the need for a feeling of achievement*. "The act of producing something of his own gives a child a feeling of confidence and achievement." Oldsters also face this need. For many of them, life is programmed, monitored, and guided by us. They need opportunities to create, express themselves, and produce something tangible that they enjoy and that others may admire.

The city of Austin sponsors an annual fair featuring handicrafts produced by its senior citizens. RSVP holds an annual banquet honoring its senior volunteers, giving them plaques and pins and special recognition. Some nursing homes proudly display art work and other crafts made by residents.

We must keep looking for new ways to dispel frustration and to foster confidence and achievement in those we love.

12
Money and the Law

Responsibility for your aging loved one includes financial and legal responsibility—something most of us would rather avoid. We don't want to know about our loved ones' financial affairs, particularly when they are still living. It seems like meddling or an intrusion on their privacy.

Parents may be close-mouthed about their financial resources or condition; often this is due to their desire to live on without being a burden and have something left over as a legacy. If you have brothers and sisters or in-laws, the possibility for further misunderstanding always exists where financial matters are concerned.

Nevertheless, when a loved one no longer can manage

his or her own affairs conveniently and competently, someone has to take charge.

I am not qualified to give legal advice, but I will mention a few areas about which you should have concern, seek legal opinion, and take some action.

Secure professional guidance. There are books dealing with family law and estate matters that you can borrow from your library. There is an excellent "Consumer Survival Kit" (related to the PBS-TV series) on law called *Advise and Represent*. Consult with your attorney.

Securing a Lawyer

Ask friends or neighbors about lawyers who have helped them, particularly in matters affecting older persons.

Call your local bar association for assistance. Usually you will be given several names.

Consult the Martindale-Hubbell Legal Directory, found in most public libraries. This multi-volume directory lists lawyers by city and state, gives their age, educational background, years of practice, specialties, and a rating. Not every lawyer is rated, and an absence of rating does not mean the lawyer is inexperienced or incompetent. Check the names you have gathered with the directory.

Telephone for an appointment, verifying the cost of a consultation fee. Discuss your needs (and costs) and decide whether you wish to hire this particular attorney.

Medical Benefits

Government medical assistance programs vary from country to country (and state to state within a country). In the

United States we have *Medicare* and *Medicaid*.

Medicare becomes available at age 65, usually when Social Security payments begin. It is a form of health co-insurance with deductibles, with premiums deducted from Social Security payments. Medicare does not cover all medical costs. A hefty up-front payment of several hundred dollars is required with hospitalization. Presently only 80 percent of approved surgery is covered. The remainder must be paid from savings or private insurance plans; "Medigap" insurance is available for this purpose.

Medicaid is medical insurance for those who do not qualify for Medicare. For some people, it begins where Medicare leaves off. Such persons may not receive any Social Security benefits, but do get Supplemental Security Income (SSI). Medicaid is available for the disabled of any age—not just 65 and older. Medicaid is financed by the federal and state governments and is administered by state welfare agencies; however, it is not of itself a "welfare program." Eligibility is carefully defined. A person may own a house, a car (up to a certain value), and a prepaid burial plot and funeral plan but cannot have cash assets above established amounts.

Specific financial benefits and guidelines change from year to year. Contact your local Social Security office for current leaflets and other information about Medicare and Medicaid.

Nursing Home Costs

Nursing home costs are high and climbing. The fee includes meals and usually laundry. Many nursing homes continue to charge a daily rate, sometimes reduced, while a resident is temporarily in a hospital; this insures that a bed will still be available when that resident returns to the nursing home. When you multiply the daily rate by 365 days, the annual cost can be frightening.

Money Matters

Inflation may have its greatest impact upon the lives of the elderly. It affects their fixed incomes and their savings. Medical health care costs were never higher and will likely increase. Housing costs are considered the second greatest problem of the elderly.

Evaluate your loved one's economic situation, make adjustments and judgments, and do your best to stretch those resources so that care and comfort will be provided. Know that you may have to make up the difference or find some other way to manage when your loved one's resources are exhausted. Longevity affects economics, which affects each of us. And it will have a still greater impact upon our children.

Your chief goal ought to be liquidity. Long-term investments are especially attractive in a time of inflation, but sufficient cash must be available to pay bills.

I maintained a separate checking account and two savings accounts for Paul. One savings account was a regular passbook account; withdrawals could be made at any time. The other account was a six-month certificate-of-deposit (or "money-market") account that earned more interest but didn't tie up Paul's money for any long period of time.

I maintained only a passbook savings account for Anna. Carolyn co-signed for these accounts; if anything happened to me, she could have managed the financial affairs of both parents without waiting for a court determinatioin of settlement.

These separate accounts facilitated my bookkeeping. I easily verified all receipts and expenditures, since all checks and other income sent to Paul or Anna were immediately deposited.

The savings accounts were trust accounts; they bore the Social Security number of either Paul or Anna. Interest was credited to them, not to me, and was reported to the Internal Revenue Service.

Paul had Social Security benefits, a small pension, a continuing small stipend from a supporting church. Interest from investments paid about 65 percent of his monthly expenses. The remainder came from his savings, supplemented by the family.

Paul had no commercial or governmental securities. He owned no life insurance. His investments were in bonds—several could not be cashed in without substantial loss, so they provided limited convertible assets.

So a standard safe and easy policy for inexperienced investors like myself was to stay with reliable savings institutions that were federally insured.

Legal Adjustments
How may the affairs of a disabled or handicapped loved one best be handled? Let's look at a few legal terms.

A Trust. A simple trust can be drawn, naming a friend, a family member, or a banking institution as trustee. The trustee's obligations are defined. Property transferred to the trustee is used for the care and protection of the loved one. Upon the loved one's death, property is distributed as the trust instructs. Regular accounting is required. The trust may be revoked at any time by the loved one. A lawyer must be consulted to devise a trust that may require only official recording in the court to become operative.

A trust may be drawn only if the loved one is lucid and alert and is only physically disabled.

Guardianship. If the loved one is mentally incompetent and unable to designate a trustee, then the court appoints a guardian or a conservator—someone the family recommends or someone the court feels can serve best in this capacity. A lawyer advises and draws up the required petition.

Power of Attorney. This is authorization for someone to act on another's behalf. A loved one may grant general authority to someone to handle all his affairs. Or he may authorize specific authority, such as opening a checking account or selling securities or property.

Some lawyers advise against using power of attorney, pointing out that authorization is valid only as long as the maker is competent. The authorization also ends with the maker's, or grantor's, death.

You can buy standard power-of-attorney forms in a legal stationery store. I did just that before flying up to St. Paul to see Paul after his stroke. I also consulted a couple of family law books and my attorney before I left. I took the form with me for Paul to sign.

The hospital business manager was convinced that Paul understood and agreed with the provisions. He and another person witnessed Paul's "x," and I became Paul's limited agent, his "attorney-in-fact." This allowed me to handle such matters as his banking affairs, cashing his bonds upon maturity, and selling his car.

Although I see the necessity for trusteeships and guardianships, I believe the power of attorney is a valuable and essential first step. Some states allow the possibility of a power of attorney taking effect only with the disability of the "principal"; thus, it can be prepared in advance of any real need. Also, powers of attorney can specify a date when the power will end. If the principal becomes incompetent, some states do allow the power of attorney to continue. Other states make quick provision for temporary guardianship.

Executor. This is the person named in a will to carry out its provisions. If you are named, you are free to serve or to decline. It would be helpful to discuss the matter with the lawyer who drew up the will.

The list of responsibilities of an executor is long, dealing with matters of probate, creditors, taxes, and distribution of assets. Such lists may be available from your library, lawyer, insurance agent, or mortician.

Check with your local Internal Revenue Service office about required forms and declarations for executors.

Representative Payee. This is a Social Security term

describing someone who serves as an agent in receiving and depositing Social Security checks. You can apply for representative payee status at your local Social Security office, where you can also obtain an excellent guide on procedures.

Legal Counsel

Consult with your attorney about contractual matters, such as an agreement with a nursing home, an insurance policy, a complicated transfer of property, or a careful review of a "life care" retirement center contract.

When issuers of bonds default or declare bankruptcy, you will need legal representation to follow through on the hearings and advise you on the various plans of settlement that may be offered.

If your loved one hasn't made a will, bring your loved one and a lawyer together for this purpose. Preparing a will is not expensive, and it doesn't have to be complicated. A "letter of instructions" indicating disposition of household effects and other wishes can be stated informally; this does not have to be part of the will.

Wills don't have to be drawn up in a lawyer's office; they are valid if properly witnessed. John B. Kelly, Princess Grace's father, was a maverick millionaire who wrote his own will. He didn't like legal jargon so he began his will this way: "This is my last will and testament and I believe I am of sound mind. Some lawyers will question this when they read my will; however, I have my opinion of some of them, so that makes us even." His will wasn't questioned, but personally, I'd rather not gamble.

Consult a lawyer about certain liabilities involving your loved one's care. Someone may be injured in your home while assisting him. Nursing homes are always nervous about their liability and require release forms from next of kin regarding bed rails and physical restraints. Whenever injury or property damage is involved, a lawyer can help sort out facts and regulations and advise you accordingly.

A new area for litigation may emerge in the field of "patient rights." Nursing homes are legally required to inform residents of these rights upon their admission. They deal with the patient's right to participate in the planning of his own treatment, to be kept medically informed, and to be assured of confidentiality concerning medical information. When the resident becomes incompetent, the next of kin ought to become the loved one's agent and should be kept similarly informed. This is not happening as often as it should, and the denial of these rights may have to be tested in the courts.

Insurance

If your loved one carries no life insurance, investigate the possibility of purchasing a small policy, perhaps one that will cover funeral expenses.

Even term policies are expensive (and sometimes not available after age seventy-five). You must judge whether

they offer sufficient value for the premium. Blue Cross/
Blue Shield sometimes offers life insurance policies to
senior citizens, as does the insurance affiliate of AARP.

Taxes

Depending on your loved one's income, you may be required to file an income tax return for him or her. It may
also be necessary to file a "final" return upon his or her
death. In all cases you must inform the Social Security
office of the death of a loved one who has been receiving
benefits.

Your caregiving may also affect your own return. You
may claim an exemption if a parent or some other older
relative lives with you, for whom you provide more than
half of that person's support. If other members of your
family share in those costs, any member who provides at
least ten percent of the dependent's support may claim
the exemption. Only one member can make this claim in
any given year. There can be a rotation of such annual
claims where several family members participate in support.

Consult your local IRS office or your attorney for current and specific information. Ask about tax information
for survivors, executors, and administrators, as well as
the "multiple support declaration."

Social Security

You must apply for Social Security benefits—those
monthly checks just don't begin to arrive automatically.

Your loved one should apply at the nearest Social Security office, either in person or by telephone. Find the address and phone number in your telephone book under "United States Government."

Reduced benefits are available as early as age sixty-two. Full benefits begin at age sixty-five. Apply three months before the date you wish the benefits to begin.

Application for Medicare is made through your local Social Security office as well. This is also where you apply for "representative payee" status, if required.

Food Stamps

This program is helpful to qualified elderly persons who live independently or in certain home-care situations. Food stamps extend and expand a limited food budget.

Food stamps are a program of the U.S. Department of Agriculture but are usually administered in individual states by welfare or human services departments. Consult these offices for current information.

Discounts

Discounts help senior citizens to stretch budgets.

Banks often waive monthly charges for checking accounts.

Bus lines (city and interstate) and airlines offer reduced fare rates.

Department stores and drug stores sometimes advertise a 10 or 15 percent discount to persons sixty-five or older— a large savings when prescription drugs are needed.

Some cafeterias and restaurants promote senior citizen discounts.

Many state museums, art galleries, theaters, and concert series offer discounts to those over sixty-five.

Personal Identification

Every person needs some kind of official identification to cash checks or establish new accounts. The most widely accepted identification is a driver's license, but some older people do not have these. County offices and many city police departments now provide an official ID card with a photograph, for older persons who no longer drive. Usually these are free.

Voter Registration

Your loved one may still want to participate actively in the democratic process. Keeping up with political campaigns—both national and local—is another way to keep up with reality.

Check with your county registration office about deadlines for registration. If your parent is unable to write, you (the son or daughter) are allowed to register and sign for your parent. Your parent may then vote in person or by absentee ballot, which you can request from your city clerk.

Con Games and Other Forms of Exploitation

The elderly are still considered fair game by unscrupulous entrepreneurs.

Your local Better Business Bureau has pamphlets and current information about the more common rackets operating in your city or county.

If your loved ones live independently, alert them to such dangers.

Under no circumstances should your loved one ever withdraw savings from a bank or savings-and-loan association at a stranger's request.

If your loved one is ever approached with any kind of scheme, he or she should get in touch with you or the police as soon as possible.

Your loved one should be wary of any home improvement "specials" offered by door-to-door salespersons. Inferior materials are used or the job is never completed, but usually the price has been paid in advance to people with no local address. Repairs should be made by local firms who are willing to provide references and performance bonds. Checking with the Better Business Bureau or the Chamber of Commerce on persons soliciting work is also helpful.

Most cities require licenses for any door-to-door solicitation for business or charity. Encourage your loved ones to ask for the appropriate I.D.

Your loved ones should be aware that if they sign a contract in their home for any merchandise, they have the legal right to cancel that contract within three days.

Sometimes unordered merchandise is received through the mail, followed by bills and letters. Often these are tied in with appeals for charities. Lots of greeting cards or handicrafts by supposed "native Americans" or "war-displaced refugees" are distributed in this way. So are books and raffle tickets. Such mailings are speculation on the part of the mailer. If the item was not ordered, it doesn't have to be paid for nor returned.

Estate Planning

Several elements of estate planning have been mentioned, but some review and expansion might be helpful.

If your loved one is wealthy, estate planning has probably already begun or is in process. However, even where large cash reserves or property holdings and investment portfolios do not exist, consider alternatives that affect inheritance taxes. There may also be ways we can help ourselves as we approach our own retirement years.

In 1790, a member of the U.S. Congress is reported to have said that "the time will come when the poor man will not be able to wash his shirt without paying a tax."

"Death taxes" do exist. The federal government calls them "estate taxes." Most states call them "inheritance taxes."

There is a floor or limit below which such taxes are not levied. No such taxes were paid by any of Paul's or Anna's heirs; Paul's and Anna's resources were too limited. However, remember that inflation has greatly increased the value of real estate. A residence or farm that was purchased years ago by your loved one for several thousand dollars may now be valued in the six figures.

Whether we like it or not, we have to concern ourselves with estate matters.

State inheritance laws vary and do not always follow federal guidelines. If property is owned in several states, taxes for each state may be required.

Both federal and state laws insist that appropriate reports be filed within a year after death whether or not any tax is due. Tax courts can be petitioned for an extension if "hardship" can be proved.

Since estate laws are complicated, consult an attorney who specializes in estate planning and inheritance tax laws.

Consider these areas:

Estate and inheritance taxes can be minimized; the law provides for this. These aren't tax "loopholes"; they are provisions the government expects its citizens to claim.

Distinction is made between "separate" and "community" property. When a spouse dies, all "separate" property is subject to tax, while only half of "community" property is considered part of the estate.

There are laws that allow for marital deductions, or special large gifts made during the lifetime of both spouses.

The estate can also be reduced during one's lifetime by making certain gifts to friends or relatives.

A loved one might choose to make a gift of property to a family member or to a charitable organization. The gift would be taxed if given to an individual, but the tax would be based upon the market value of the property at the time of the gift. In an era of continuing inflation, it can be safely predicted that gift taxes on property will be less if paid *now* rather than paid *later* as estate taxes. Consult your attorney or accountant.

Your loved ones might want to consider making larger contributions to missions organizations or churches or other charitable groups.

Earlier we talked about trusts. These can be "revocable" or "irrevocable," and they can help others while providing tax relief for the donor. Trusts should be established with the help of a professional.

Beneficiaries should be named in insurance policies as well as in mutual funds where allowable, and pension plans. Depending on the amount, insurance proceeds received by an individual may not be taxable. However, if they or similar proceeds are merely assigned to the "estate," estate and inheritance taxes will apply.

Most people want to leave something to someone else at the time of their death. Talk frankly about such hopes and wishes while your loved ones are still living.

Regardless of your loved one's resources, he can do more good with funds and property now than later. Make sure your loved one realizes this fact of tax life in our economic system.

Another point to consider is liquidity or availability of funds. If it is known that estate and inheritance taxes will have to be paid, those taxes must be paid by a certain date and from resources in hand. Some funds should be readily available to the executor or administrator within a six-month period after death if property or securities are not to be prematurely sold, perhaps at a loss, merely to satisfy a tax lien.

Finances are a sensitive area of family life. Overcome your own misgivings and reluctance about discussing decisions concerning money or property. Marshall your facts, secure the professional advice you need, and risk the possible or imagined indictment of being self-serving.

By facing these realities soon enough, you'll be doing a service for your loved one and for those people and causes about which your loved one has continuing concern.

13
Funeral Arrangements

Today there is more open discussion about death and dying, and that is truly a hopeful sign. Christians, especially, should never be reluctant to discuss death, not if their faith is real and trusting. There can be no resurrection of the body without the death of the body.

Talk about Death
As your loved ones grow older, it's *essential* that you talk through the implications of death and their preferences regarding a funeral service and burial. First, talk through your own and your loved one's attitudes about death and the future life.

Talk about Wishes

When it's time to discuss specifics, you'll want to talk with your loved one about his or her will. This doesn't have to be a morbid or self-serving exercise. If he hasn't made a will and is mentally capable of doing so, encourage your loved one to prepare one with the help of a lawyer.

If your loved one has made a will, find out the name of the lawyer who drew it, the location of the original, and who was named executor. The original copy of a will should not be kept in a safe-deposit box because these are usually sealed for several days (or weeks) by the court following death. A *copy* of the will might be kept in a safe-deposit box, but the original should be in the hands of a lawyer, the executor, or a family member.

Discuss your loved one's wishes for the disposition of special possessions that are not mentioned in the will—things like a stamp collection, a piano, or a favorite chair. Then write it in a letter, have your loved one sign it, and keep it with the original copy of the will. Such a letter could also contain specific instructions for the funeral.

Talk about the Funeral

Take time to plan a funeral or memorial service together. Read through one of the standard services found in the *Minister's Star Book* or in the manual of your church. While it is true that funeral services are for the living, we rarely take time to read the Scriptures and prayers of a funeral service with our deaths in mind. Such a review can be a powerful moment for renewed and strengthened faith, for finding new courage, and for affirming our hope.

Your loved one may be dissatisfied with a standard service; in that case, write your own service together. What music should you have (a favorite hymn sung by the congregation, or by a soloist or a choir)? What favorite Scriptures should be included? Should there be an affirmation of faith, such as a congregational reciting of the Apostles' Creed? What does your loved one want to say to friends and family who will be present? The process of developing a funeral service together can be a marvelous devotional experience as well as a practical decision for the future.

I have attended many glorious funeral services that left me inspired and happy. A funeral can be a tremendous testimony and affirmation of faith, not only to those who believe but also to non-Christians who are present for the service.

The "Where" and "How" of Burial

Find out where your loved one wishes to be buried. Is it close by? Beside a spouse, perhaps long since deceased and buried in a distant cemetery? Has a burial plot already been purchased?

Does your loved one wish to be buried? Has cremation been considered? This has theological as well as economic implications. Cremation is a clean, orderly method of returning the body to the elements. Except for two states (Massachusetts and Michigan), a casket is not required if cremation is done immediately.

Embalming is not required if cremation is done within

twenty-four hours after death. However, embalming is necessary if the body is to be viewed or transported a distance for burial. Embalming restores the body of a loved one to a more natural state.

Ground burial is expensive because of the cost of land. In most cemeteries, ground burial now requires the additional expense of a concrete liner to protect the solid surface of the lawn.

Discuss with your loved one how his religious convictions might affect accepted cultural practices. Ask whether the service should be held in a funeral chapel (where you will be charged) or a Christian church. Should there be a graveside service? A memorial service instead of a funeral? Memorial services are held when the body is not present due to accident, cremation, disposition to a medical school, or simply by the wish of the deceased one.

If your loved one has been active and well known or has lived and worked in several different locations, you may want to discuss the possibility of one or more memorial services in other cities.

The "Living Will"

Discuss the making of a "Living Will." If a person is terminally ill, he or she may not wish to be kept alive by so-called "heroic" measures. Living Wills are not legally binding instruments in every state, but they do carry moral and personal weight.

The following is a sample text of a "Living Will." (You may secure copies of this revised edition from *Concern for Dying*).

*To My Family, My Physician, My Lawyer
and All Others Whom It May Concern*

Death is as much a reality as birth, growth, maturity, and old age—it is the one certainty of life. If the time comes when I can no longer take part in decisions for my own future, let this statement stand as an expression of my wishes and directions, while I am still of sound mind.

If at such a time the situation should arise in which there is no reasonable expectation of my recovery from extreme physical or mental disability, I direct that I be allowed to die and not be kept alive by medications, artificial means, or "heroic measures." I do, however, ask that medication may be mercifully administered to me to alleviate suffering, even though this may shorten my remaining life.

This statement is made after careful consideration and is in accordance with my strong convictions and beliefs. I want the wishes and directions here expressed carried out to the extent permitted by law. Insofar as they are not legally enforceable, I hope that those to whom this Will is addressed will regard themselves as morally bound by these provisions.

Here one may insert specific statements, if desired, such as who is appointed to make binding decisions concerning medical treatment, mention of specific measures of artificial life support, the preference to live out last days at home if this does not jeopardize recovery to a meaningful, perceptive life or impose an undue burden on one's family, and any reference to donating tissues and organs as transplants.

The statement is then signed, dated, and witnessed by two persons. Several people should receive a copy, including your physician. A person should review, initial, and date this document annually to make it evident that this statement represents his or her continuing intent.

Donations

Many people now consider willing their bodies to medical schools for research or donating specific organs, such as eyes or kidneys, to organ "banks." A uniform donor card is available that is considered to be a legally binding will. It should be carried by the donor at all times. Additional information can be secured by writing to the *American Medical Association,* the *Living Bank,* or the *Concern for Dying Educational Council* (see Resources at the end of this book).

You might want to discuss whether your loved one has a special charity, ministry, or mission program to which contributions might be made in lieu of flowers.

Wheelchairs and other medical equipment might be given to a nursing home or to your church.

Our Parenting Decisions

In Anna's case, we waited too long to discuss funeral plans with her—she became confused and unaware. But Carolyn and I had several conversations with Paul. He made it clear that if he died in Ecuador, he wanted to be buried there. (Anyone traveling overseas should carry some statement about such wishes. In the case of death or accident overseas, the normal procedure is for the U.S. consul to return the body to the United States.)

Paul also made it clear that if he died in the United States, he wanted to be buried next to his wife Bernice in Mt. Gilead, Ohio, where a family plot was already purchased. Because of this wish, we knew he wanted ground burial and to be embalmed.

We knew which hymns Paul wanted sung at his memorial and graveside service and that he wanted costs kept to a minimum. He preferred that friends contribute to missions or the cause of distributing Scriptures instead of purchasing flowers.

Carolyn and I made arrangements on the basis of this knowledge. We secured burial contracts for both Paul and Anna and chose the type of casket. We knew the exact costs in advance. We discussed financial obligations and a schedule of payment with our mortician.

There were many advantages to making these decisions in advance—we could decide intelligently and calmly, without being pressured; we could find a mortician sympathetic to our wishes and objectives. And if our parents had outlived Carolyn or me, plans for their funerals would be on file at each nursing home and could easily be carried out by someone else.

Here is how those plans worked out.

A memorial service was held for Paul in Cleveland in the church he once served and which supported him over the years. We followed the order and sang the hymns Paul had approved months earlier. Graveside services were held for both Paul and Anna. Paul was buried in Mt. Gilead, near Cleveland. Anna was buried in Justice, Illinois, next to her husband. Her service was bilingual, in English and Lithuanian, as she would have wished.

Other Details

Most states now have chapters of "Memorial Societies"— voluntary groups of people who seek to obtain dignity, simplicity, and economy in funeral arrangements through advance planning. You might find help from one of these.

Check on special death benefits that may be available to your loved one from Social Security or the Veterans Administration. Medicare pays for final medical bills. Unions, pension funds, insurance, fraternal orders, and professional groups may also have special benefits to offer. If the cause of death was related to employment, workmen's compensation may allow certain death benefits.

When a loved one dies, you will want to notify immediate family, close friends, and business colleagues by phone. Having a list in advance helps. More distant friends can be informed by letter. Notify insurance companies. Cancel automobile insurance.

Arrange for family members or close friends to take turns answering the door or telephone, and keep a record of calls.

Write an obituary that could be sent to your loved one's college alumni publication and/or other journals and newspapers where friends will learn about the death.

Check on debts. Some may be covered by credit insurance. It is helpful to have adequate and accurate financial records about your loved one's business affairs.

Finally, a word about grave markers.

My father designed his own monument, which he intended to be a continuing reminder of his mission in life. He wanted an open Bible to show the words of John 3:16. Anna and I kept faith with his wish, and the monument stands in the Lithuanian National Cemetery in Justice, Illinois.

Markers can be expensive, and sometimes unscrupulous sales tactics are used to pressure family members into buying something elaborate and expensive. Cemeteries—especially those providing so-called "perpetual care"—have grave marker requirements that limit material, size, and style.

Perhaps your loved one has something special to say in this visible, public way.

Benjamin Franklin did. This is his self-written epitaph.

The Body
of
Benjamin Franklin, Printer
(Like the cover of an old book,
its contents torn out,
And stripped of its lettering and gilding)
Lies here food for worms.
Yet the work itself shall not be lost,

For it will (as he believes) appear once
more
In a new
And beautiful Edition
Corrected and Amended
by
The Author

14
Visiting and Communicating with Elderly People

During her last three years Anna rarely recognized me as her son. She accepted Carolyn and was grateful for her attention, but she didn't know Carolyn as her daughter-in-law. Paul always recognized us for who we were to him. He identified his grandchildren and great-grandchildren from the pictures on his wall. Most of the time he could receive information, but he couldn't always respond because his speaking vocabulary was limited by aphasia.

Anna and Paul both lived with severe communication handicaps. But we discovered that it is often just as difficult to communicate with disabled people who are neither senile nor disoriented nor affected by a speech disorder. Why? Because depression is the primary emotional ailment. Like pain or disability, it can hinder the process of communication. But when older loved ones are lonely, bewildered with their surroundings, enduring discomfort, suffering pain, and perhaps trying to cope with a frustrating handicap, those are the times visits can be most helpful and meaningful.

Here are a few suggestions for relating to older friends and loved ones, particularly those who live in nursing homes or other institutions.

Reality Orientation
Social workers recommend that older people be "kept in touch" by way of "reality orientation" or "reality therapy," a fancy name for a rather simple procedure, to establish some sense of reality and personhood for your loved one.

Whenever you visit a loved one who is becoming more confused about himself and life, turn the conversation to some reality. Establish what day and date it is (calendars are helpful). Ask the person his or her name; if possible, get your loved one to write it. Discuss the season of the year and the weather outside. Underscore where the loved one is living—in what city and in what state, as well as the name of the nursing home. You might want to chat about some headline of the day. Call attention to upcoming anniversaries and family pictures. Repeat these kinds of reality questions during each visit. It isn't childish or irrelevant. However, remember—not every resident of a nursing home suffers from brain damage or some handicap that restricts communication. For those who are blessed with clear minds, conversation is no problem. All you need to do is ask a question about a home town or a garden or grandchildren, and you can sit back and listen.

Negotiation and Forgiveness

I strongly believe that elderly people should be treated as adults and not as children. However, this is easier to believe than to practice, particularly when senility brings on *childlike* (not necessarily *childish*) behavior.

It's also difficult to maintain this adult-to-adult relationship if we assume the role of being parent for our parent.

There may be a need for *negotiation* in this new relationship for both of you. It may be necessary to make clear that you are no longer a child and that your parent is no longer a parent in the way he or she once experienced that role. Treating each other and visiting each other as *adults* will help establish a foundation for this new kind of family partnership.

It's essential to come to new understandings in this emerging relationship with our parents—in other words, to negotiate—because we as children carry so much emotional baggage with us.

We remember our parents as they used to be. Perhaps we still think of ourselves as we used to be. We remember past slights and misunderstandings and instances of our own erratic behavior. We remember things we said and situations that haunt us. We need to forgive our parents, and often we may feel that our parents still need to forgive us.

Perhaps we can discuss these things with our parents. On the other hand, the event that sears our memory may long since have been erased from theirs. This is when we must negotiate with our Creator, who knows us and our relationships. If we are to establish healthy, supportive ties with our aging parents, we must turn over our residual or actual guilt and anger to God. He does forgive and He does heal. Only in this way can we go forward.

Persons of Worth and Dignity

While your loved one is still alert and involved with life, remember that you are the *visitor* to his or her residence. But when loved ones are confused or handicapped, it's often necessary to "take charge." In whatever you do, protect older people's dignity, for it is fragile.

Be Consistent and Regular

Maintaining a definite schedule doesn't mean you always have to visit on Mondays at four; there will be times when you'll need to visit on Tuesdays at noon instead. But remember, some elderly people are quite conscious of time and the clock (Paul was one of these). Regularity is important, whether you visit in person or by telephone, letter, or cassette tape. Don't give up visiting merely because visiting is difficult. Without your visit your loved one would become more withdrawn and more depressed. You don't visit to be appreciated; you visit to demonstrate by your presence that you still care, to be of whatever help and support you can be.

A Few Suggestions for Visits

1. *Take advantage of nostalgia.* Prepare a book of snapshots relating to your loved one's life. Ask for explanations or descriptions, and write these under the pictures. This could become a kind of "This-Is-Your-Life" album that you can review whenever you visit, and that your loved one will find captivating and amusing when alone. This is good reality orientation as well. Perhaps staff members will enjoy seeing it and getting to know your loved one better.

An old magazine—one that's thirty or forty years old—can sometimes serve the same purpose. Looking at old advertisements and pictures, seeing the old styles and old cars, can trigger happy memories. The recently reprinted *1908 Sears Catalog* makes a great gift!

2. *Get your parent or loved one to talk about those memories.* When did Mother meet Father, and how? Where was their first home? What was it like? Build on past interest in sports or hobbies or vocation. Get your loved one to talk; one of the best things you can do as a visitor is to listen. Patients are constantly being told what to do and where to go, and they don't have much opportunity to chat.

Bring a map with you once in a while—perhaps one of the United States or the world. Let your loved one point out those states where he or she lived, or the countries visited.

Bring a tape cassette recorder with you. Preserve this

oral history for yourself, your children, and your children's children. We had done some of this with Paul before his stroke, on those occasions when he visited us. He also left us voluminous journals of his early work in Ecuador (these are now in the Billy Graham Center archives in Wheaton, Illinois). With the memories of Paul's surviving family and friends, we know a great deal about him. It is so different with Anna. There is no surviving family other than myself. There is so much I do not know, that I wish I had asked her, while there was still time.

3. *Share some exercise.* A walk down the corridor is always helpful; outdoors is better if the weather cooperates. If your loved one is handicapped, massage unused muscles.

4. *Work on a gift together.* There may be a small craft item you could work on for a grandchild's or great-grandchild's birthday. You can choose from easy-to-make, economical leathercraft items, simple embroidery items, or paint-by-number posters. Working together can be fun, and the project might occupy part of several visits. If you are between projects, bring a simple puzzle along.

5. *Bring something to read.* If your loved one is aphasic or withdrawn, remember that if you can't chat, you can at least read. Bring something that will hold interest and that can be read in small segments with each visit. While cassette tapes of many fine books are available through libraries, your personal reading of an old favorite will bring special pleasure. Reading can provide structure and substance to your visits. (Pastors might keep this simple hint in mind.)

6. *Memorize a joke or two, and share these*. Visits among church-related people like Paul and Anna sometimes tended to be overly somber and even pompous. There is precious little laughter in the lives of the sick and the handicapped. Bring back some joy into their lives. Carolyn and I have found the *Reader's Digest* invaluable for short articles, anecdotes, and humorous stories.

7. *When you speak, you don't necessarily have to shout*. Sometimes we think every older person is deaf.

8. *Be prepared to be silent*. Planning things to do or say is desirable, but your visit won't be a disaster if nothing is said or done. Your loved one may be drowsy or may not be feeling well. Or both of you may suddenly be caught up with past memories.

This is when tactile communication—speaking by way of touch—is needed. I said very little to Anna as I pushed her wheelchair up and down the corridor or outside her building. There was little we could say to each other, but I massaged her back, I held her hand, I brushed her hair. The silent times were many.

Paul often seemed content to be left alone. He needed time to be alone, to meditate, to pray, or just to doze. It was his privilege.

Your loved one may be morose, despondent, and withdrawn. At times you may even sense resentment. Accept these silent moods. All these things will pass. Be content with the "now." Some older people may remember more of the distant past than the immediate past; they may remember little, if anything, of what transpired yesterday. But they do experience the immediate moment. The present is the common denominator, so enjoy it.

9. *Be bright.* Many things may be going wrong in the world, in your family, or perhaps even in your perception of the quality of care being given to your loved one. I don't believe that a visit is the appropriate time or place to ventilate such concerns. If your loved one raises questions about family or care, then of course they should be faced and answered. But don't overload your kin with a lot of unnecessary worries or concerns. I certainly would avoid criticizing institutional staff or administration in front of patients. Such problems should be dealt with at the level where solutions are achievable, not where anxieties will be increased.

Be satisfied with the act of visiting. No great emotional, intellectual, physical, or spiritual breakthrough may occur. If it does, thank God for the serendipity—and return another time expecting again only the opportunity of being together for this particular and immediate moment.

10. *Those of us who are Christians find special strength in reading Scripture and praying together.* I wish we would always feel free to pray. Not only is this valid "reality orientation," but it is precisely at such times that one can sense God's Spirit close by.

11. *Make your visit brief.* Sometimes it will be obvious that you shouldn't stay longer than ten minutes. Other times, things may go well for half an hour. Don't overdo and don't overextend. Leave something unsaid or incomplete for the next visit. In my view, short, frequent visits are much better than long, occasional ones.

12. *Get to know some of your loved one's friends in the nursing home and visit them.* Meet the relatives of those friends. Perhaps, in time, you could trade off visits, adding visitors to your loved one and his friends. This could prove helpful if you are away on vacation or caught in an emergency and you need someone to look in on your loved one.

There are many lonely souls in nursing homes who have no one to visit them. We can't carry the entire burden, but there may be one or two people besides our loved ones who need us as a friend.

Gift Giving

Gifts do not have to be limited to anniversaries and birthdays. In fact, sometimes the significance of these occasions is diminished for older persons. But the excitement of opening a gaily wrapped package never totally disappears.

Make a special event of giving a needed item of clothing—a new dressing gown or pair of pajamas, a colorful flannel shirt for colder days, or perhaps a pair of slippers. Give dusting powder, lightly scented spray cologne or shaving lotion.

One rose from your garden can bring delight. A growing plant—preferably one that will blossom—also makes a good gift. A more active older person might enjoy a flowerpot with potting soil, a tulip bulb, or some seeds.

Practical gifts might include a "blanket support"—a device to support a blanket over the feet, giving more room for movement—or a tray table that fits over the arms of a wheelchair. A massage unit would make a practical and therapeutic gift.

Mobiles that turn and reflect light, pictures, large photographs of family members, and posters decorate a room and provide pleasant moments of diversion and thought.

Tabletop radios with easy-to-handle controls, cassette recorders, or a window fan also make good gifts. If a television is not readily available, a personal TV set— preferably one in color and with a remote control device— would be a long-term, ongoing gift.

Visiting Is Your Responsibility

The burden of visiting your loved one in a nursing home is yours and possibly yours alone. If your loved one lives with you at home, whatever socialization occurs will most likely depend on what you design and engineer.

"Burden" may seem a harsh word, but I think it's reality. It doesn't have to mean hardship or vexing obligation. It can be light—a challenge and opportunity for growing compassion. But the responsibility also becomes tedious and frustrating. We must recognize this fact in order to deal with it.

Trust Your Instincts

The threshold of pain and frustration is easily lowered as we review check lists, listen to suggestions, and read books such as this one. We feel we should consult the experts—and even our friends.

But we live with a daily reality that doesn't always conveniently fit the categories we read about. It's easy to become bewildered and to feel guilty. Since the responsibility is ours, there may come a time when we have to square our shoulders and do it our way, risking setbacks and perhaps even failure, but finding some strength and confidence in the knowledge we have gained about our own loved ones. In other words, trust your instincts.

For example, some experts claim that one-to-one visits are best, that when there is more than one visitor, the closeness of two people conversing and sharing is lost. But Carolyn and I have visited our parents (and other friends in hospitals and nursing homes) together, and we have not sensed that a diverse climate was created.

Here's another example: Well-meaning friends can throw you a curve. They don't often visit your loved ones, but when they do they'll telephone to report. Of course this is thoughtful, but there's a problem—friends want us to feel good, so they give a positive report. Sometimes it's difficult to recognize whom they are describing!

I've said before that Paul was aphasic. Occasionally I received calls that began, "Paul is really improving; I understood almost everything he said." The first time, the call troubled me greatly. Was this person talking about the same Paul I knew? He had lived in our home for nearly two years, and we had had daily contact. Now I was visiting him several times a week. I knew *I* couldn't understand everything Paul was trying to say.

You see, conversing with Paul was often like playing

"twenty questions"—determining the subject (is it animal or vegetable?), the geography of the subject, and the time frame. I have probed and pondered for half an hour over something I thought was deeply theological or financial only to discover finally that Paul wanted some extra dollar bills in his wallet or wondered where his handkerchiefs had gone. This kind of conversation wears you out, but afterwards you laugh about it together.

I think Paul's friends were so relieved to hear an occasional understandable word from Paul that they grasped it as something symbolic, making more of it than they should. Or they were so disturbed by their inability to communicate and understand that they left after the first recognizable word, wanting to feel good after a frustrating experience.

A third example: Once you have decided on long-term care for your loved one (usually after consultation and urging from your physician), a friend with raised eyebrow may ask in a tone that sounds accusing, "Well, how *is* your Dad?" Most likely, we've misinterpreted the gesture and tone. Learn to live with the risk of some people not fully understanding your decision and misinterpreting your motives.

A final example: It's easy to be overwhelmed by the professional hierarchy in long-term health-care institutions. You can so easily be "put down" as a mere layman. If you observe conditions and practices that you question and that affect the care of your loved one, be assertive. Some things in life are too important to entrust totally to the hands of professionals. Trust your instincts.

Over the months and years, Carolyn and I acquired a sixth sense in communicating with Paul and Anna. Despite their different problems, we did reach them from time to time, and they reached out to us. Perhaps this sixth sense is really instinctive among people sharing love.

Communicating with Aphasics

Aphasia is a total or partial loss of the power to use or understand words. It is often the result of a stroke or other brain damage and presents special problems for both visitor and victim. *Expressive* aphasics are able to understand what you say; *receptive* aphasics are not. Some victims may have both kinds of impediment.

Paul was an *expressive* aphasic. We read to him, he watched television, and he tried to participate in singing and in repeating familiar Scripture passages. But he had a hard time communicating to us those feelings and words that were important to him. Sometimes we anticipated what he wanted to say, completing sentences for him without allowing him enough time to struggle with his words.

You know the feeling that a word is "on the tip of your tongue." This is the condition expressive aphasics experience most of the time!

Speech therapists attack the problem by working with phonics and those sounds the patient has greatest difficulty with. Large picture cards are used to help rebuild vocabulary. It is a slow and precise process. Some speech therapists do not welcome extra "drill work" by nonprofessionals; others encourage this, but want to direct and monitor your work.

Some aphasics use picturegram grids where they can fill in answers by pointing to the appropriate drawing. This tool did not work for Paul. To help him communicate with visitors and fellow residents, I wrote an ID card for him. We discussed the draft, and I typed the text on a three-by-five index card. (Hint: keep a spare copy.) This is the text we agreed upon:

My name is Paul Young. I was born near Pittsburgh in 1893. I accepted Christ as my Savior in my teens and felt called to serve Him. In 1918 I went to Ecuador as an evangelist and pastor. I am ordained as a Baptist minister and served with the Christian and Missionary Alliance. Later I directed the United Bible Societies' work in Ecuador.

In July, 1976, I suffered a stroke that has left me with two handicaps: a paralyzed right side and "aphasia" (a speech problem). I do understand when you speak. You will have difficulty understanding me, but as we talk together you may understand a few of my words and thoughts.

I have two daughters (and seven grandchildren and five great-grandchildren). Esther Howard lives in Columbia, Maryland. Carolyn Gillies lives nearby in Austin.

I do appreciate your visit. Talking to people has always been a big part of my life. Tell me about yourself. Tell me some news. Tell me a good joke. If you have time, I would be grateful if you would read something. Perhaps we could have a prayer together.

God bless you. And thank you.

The message, typed double-spaced, filled both sides of the card. Paul seemed happy with this conversational tool. It allowed him to tell others who he was and what was important to him. It kept him from becoming a non-person, which happens sometimes to a person who is bound to a wheelchair and unable to communicate readily. It opened opportunities to look at books or scrapbooks or mementos.

For Anna, Carolyn and I prepared a small photo album with pictures of herself and Anton, our family, her grandchildren, various places she lived during her lifetime, and some of her friends. We also typed captions beside each photograph. The album was invaluable in the nursing home; many nurses and aides looked at it and gained respect for Anna's life and accomplishments. It provided her with a measure of status and dignity she might not otherwise have enjoyed.

Visiting through Correspondence

Writing is a ministry of love and sharing. Many of the preceding suggestions for personal visits apply equally to written correspondence.

I am grateful for the small group of friends who continued to write even though they received no response from Paul or Anna except as Carolyn or I wrote to them. At least twice a year, Carolyn and I mailed some kind of communication to over one hundred of Paul's and Anna's friends. We wanted to inform them about Paul and Anna, but we also hoped our writing would result in written response. And it did.

Paul and Anna each had a dozen or so faithful friends who took time to write letters and remember anniversaries. Often a card was sent, signed by members of a prayer group or a Sunday school class or some organization with which Paul or Anna once had contact. Paul especially enjoyed trying to place names with faces in his memory.

Some of the letters were outstanding. In chatty fashion, they told of their experiences or recalled some past shared event, awakening memories and reaffirming friendships.

A few letters never should have been mailed—those that conveyed gossip, catalogued personal ailments, or questioned the goodness of God.

Of course, letters do not have to contain only "sweetness and light." There is a place for relating significant news, even something tragic or disappointing. But letter-writers should try to avoid the doom-and-gloom habit, the petty, and the irrelevant. An aging relative doesn't need modern-day Job's friends.

The White House sends birthday greetings to persons eighty years or older (and to couples celebrating fiftieth wedding anniversaries). Send your request with the name and address thirty days before the birthday or anniversary date to Greetings Office, The White House, 1600 Pennsylvania Ave., Washington, D.C. 20500.

Record Your Correspondence

Instead of writing a letter, record your voice on cassette for a personal visit.

If you've never recorded a "living letter," make a trial recording and listen to it before mailing your first tape. The microphone is a sensitive instrument even on the cheapest recorders and it may reveal more of your feelings than you realize. If you're tired and depressed, you will *sound* tired and depressed. If you're happy and enthusiastic, your smile will come through. Take your time—you'll improve with practice; everyone does.

The tapes should be conversational, lively, and brief. Imagine the person sitting in front of you as you speak. Discipline yourself by using the C-20 type of cassette, which provides ten minutes per side or a total of twenty minutes. Experiment with the idea of conversing and/or reading for five minutes or so, and then saying something like this: "Why don't we stop the tape here for today? Just leave everything the way it is, and we'll continue our visit tomorrow." Include humor, anecdotes, and perhaps a continued story or book reading.

Even though Carolyn and I visited our parents regularly, we also began to use cassettes. We recorded books that Paul could add to his listening library. In this way we could extend our visits beyond the time we were physically present.

15
Feeling Guilty?

It's been said that life begins when your children leave home and the family dog dies. We caregivers know that it isn't necessarily so.

As the frail elderly who touch our lives continue to fail and become more fragile and as we have to make more and more decisions, we may become overwhelmed by guilt—especially when we face that nursing home decision.

It would help if we weren't so *final* with our verbs. Often we say, "where (or when) will we *put* (or *place*) Mama in the nursing home?" Instead, we could say, "move" or "try out." Paul was in and out of three nursing homes, twice leaving them to return to our home. It helps to realize that many decisions can be made on a *trial* basis, that we can re-evaluate the situation, and we can make changes as these become obvious and necessary.

Sometimes guilt stems from the sense of having broken a promise to our loved ones and, perhaps, to ourselves. Despite the dictum that one should "never say *never*," we often tell a loved one, "I'll never put you in a nursing home." Then times and health situations change. Around-the-clock long-term health care for a parent may be the only choice left to a loving child. But that earlier "promise" has been broken and the caregiver feels guilty. He feels he has failed his loved one and that he deserves blame. I've listened to many people who told me that they feel they have broken God's law; that placing a loved one in a nursing home was not "honoring father and mother."

This is serious business. If not faced and dealt with, this guilt will erode and corrode your life and relationships.

Guilt sometimes takes the form of anger and lashing out at spouse, at children, or sometimes in actual elder abuse. More often, guilt takes the form of repeatedly reconstructing, re-living, and reviewing the decision— continuing to blame yourself for that broken promise. Even long after the death of that loved one, some of us continue to flagellate ourselves with the question of "what if?" *What* if I had tried something else? *What* if I had really tried to keep my loved one at home?

I believe we can deal with that kind of guilt only by

being responsible and respectful *adult* children. Note that I emphasized the word *adult*. True, we are always the biological children of our parents. But we have also matured. We are now *adults*. We have reached a new level of relationship. Adult children now relate to adult parents. It requires adjustment, but that's what living and growing is all about.

We are *responsible* adult children when we secure all of the facts and data we can. Try to secure the best medical diagnosis and prognosis you can and consult with a professional counselor if possible. Learn what is reversible and irreversible. Responsible caregivers are committed to finding the appropriate care for a loved one. What are your alternatives? What are your limits?

A tool I often use in workshops is called a "responsibility tree." There are circles on the branches for surviving grandparents (both yours and your spouse's), aunts and uncles, parents, brothers and sisters, children, and grandchildren. Space is left in the middle of this "tree" for "me" and "my spouse." Use the sample form in this book. First, write the appropriate names in the circles. Then draw lines under those persons for whom you are responsible (for emotional welfare, financial welfare, and finally daily care). Some names may be underlined three times. Then, put an asterisk beside the name of anyone on this tree who shares in these responsibilities.

The result of this exercise is a profile of your personal stress, as well as your degree of responsibility. Did you forget to list your own name? It is not unusual for persons

My Responsibility Tree

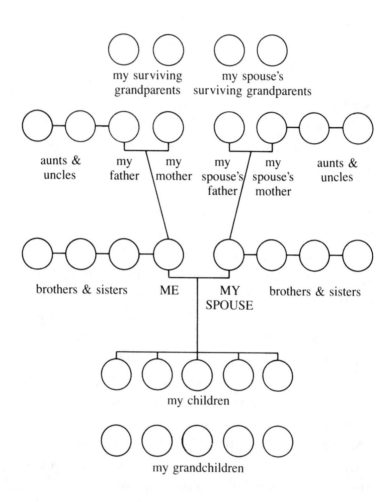

Courtesy of National Support Center for Families of the Aging

to omit their own names, thus overlooking the responsibility they have to themselves.

The "tree" illustrates those of us caught in that "sandwich generation" mentioned at the beginning of this book. Carolyn and I realized one day that not only did we have a responsibility to our *parents,* but to *ourselves,* and increasingly, to our *grandchildren.*

The National Support Center for Families of the Aging established support groups for caregivers. They have a helpful problem-solving grid that you can fill out to evaluate your caregiving situation (see next page). Three of their basic principles are relevant to this discussion about guilt:

- We realize that we cannot control all the circumstances of our lives, nor of our loved ones' lives, but we can work on our own reactions to them.
- We believe that each person in our family—including ourselves—is entitled to a fair share of our time and resources.
- We admit that we cannot produce happiness for anyone else, including our aging loved ones; nor can we expect to fill all their needs.

This is tough love—but this is the way toward guilt-free and loving decision-making. Of course it helps if your loved one can share in this decision-making process, but that isn't always possible.

I believe that if you have done your homework and

Problem-solving Grid

PROBLEM SITUATIONS	NEGATIVE FEELINGS
Type 1 *Situations Nobody Can Change*	
Type 2 *Situations Somebody Else Can Change, But Not Me*	
Type 3 *Situations with Elements I Can Change*	

Adapted from Help for Families of the Aging, *by Carol Spargo Pierskalla and Jane Dewey Heald, National Support Center for Families of the Aging, 1982.*

made a decision based upon the best knowledge and advice you can find, then you have acted responsibly.

We can be responsible and respectful adult children.

We are *respectful* when we recognize that the biological relationship continues. We can affirm our loved ones' worth and personality, despite memory loss, altered personality, or severe behavior changes. Even when we recognize that these older loved ones for whom we care may be playing games with us or manipulating us, we can still work toward preserving their dignity and striving to provide them with security and comfort.

If guilt persists, then ask for forgiveness and trust God's grace and faithfulness to forgive. As the old gospel song puts it, we should "take our burden to the Lord *and* leave it there."

Just as I trust God for my grown children, knowing there is little I can do about their problems, I must trust God for the special needs of my parents and other older loved ones. God loves them more than I ever could. We are truly in good hands.

16
Learning through Caregiving

Isn't it true that we became better parents through the process of *being* parents? Our third child had more experienced parents than our first. We can also learn to be parents of our own parents. These are the highlights of what I learned.

The Gift of Dignity
I learned that one of the greatest gifts I could give my loved ones in their declining years is the gift of dignity. Despite the winding down of body and mind, each was a person with history, values, and needs. I had to provide them as much dignity as I could in their ongoing lives and as we prepared for their deaths.

Caregiving

I learned that I was a *caregiver,* not a custodian. Providing care—or enabling someone else to provide care—was a large and gracious responsibility given to me by my Lord.

Availability

I learned that I had to be available.

I had to visit my loved ones regularly and personally. No matter how forgetful they became, they had to see and touch me, and I had to see and touch them.

This availability affected my lifestyle, but I had to accept this with grace and joy. I had to plan my trips and vacations with my loved ones in mind. It was no longer possible to place them "out of sight, out of mind." I purchased a telephone answering device not only to keep in contact with my editors and clients, but also to keep in touch with both nursing homes, wherever I went.

I had to be available for my immediate family. I had to live my own life with its responsibilities and adventures, sharing with Carolyn, our children, and our grandchildren.

Communicating

Communication has been my livelihood and profession. I have even instructed others in it. But I had to rethink my understanding of communication as I tried to communicate with my parents and other older people. I am still learning—to listen, to interpret strange sounds, to go beyond the gibberish to understand what is being conveyed through gesture and mood. In order to listen this way you have to relax, not assume too much, and be content when very little is understood.

We all speak jargon—that special language or vocabulary we use in our work and daily lives that others may not understand. Much of what we say makes little sense to people who do not share our environments or our professional interests. Thus, when I spoke to Paul about my work or a book I was reading or a seminar I had attended, I had to be careful not only that he was actually interested in the subject matter, but that he could understand the language I used to describe it.

Although I may have opened a few windows for Paul, I knew I could not change the habits of thinking and feeling he acquired through eight decades of living. Be careful not to manipulate a person who cannot verbally challenge you or argue with you. Your loved ones have not traveled your road of growth and experience; they have traveled their own. So try to listen more, to understand, to interpret, to be an occasional catalyst for a new friendship or a new idea, to innovate, to receive information, and sometimes to respond. This is the stuff of true communication.

You Are Vulnerable, Too

Today's news is frightening. International tensions of every kind threaten peace and equilibrium. I read about a future in which the trust funds of Social Security may be exhausted, about a world in which the building of schools must give way to the building of housing for increasing numbers of the elderly, most of whom may be women.

I realize that I, too, am growing old. If Alzheimer's Disease is genetic, I wonder if I am vulnerable.

I wonder if my children will have to become parents to me. They have no such obligation, of course. Nevertheless, I want them to know some of my wishes for my own latter days. I must begin to do some things for myself, looking ahead not only to retirement but also to my own death.

I want to do certain things—like get my files in order. I don't want someone else to have to wade through reams of carbon copies and boxes of slides and photographic negatives, wondering what to save and what to discard. That's something I must begin to do soon.

I hope Carolyn and I will yet be able to see those places we've read and dreamed about. If God wills it, if savings hold out, and if inflation doesn't devour us all, we will. If this doesn't come to pass, we have already been blessed with an enormous amount of travel, so we'll just relax and remember.

Of course, I must not assume too much. Unless we die together in an accident or a disaster, it's likely that one of us will survive the other. And there is the looming shadow of institutionalization. Neither of us possesses an ironclad guarantee that all will be well and serene.

Within the framework of my own vulnerability, I can only hope and trust the God I have followed. I hope I will be given the grace to continue to think, to read, and to write. If dependency comes, I hope it will be brief and not a burden to anyone. And in that process of caring for Paul and Anna with Carolyn beside me, as well as in the writing of this book, I hope I have learned something I can apply to my own life.

Returning to the Source
Our Judeo-Christian tradition commands us to honor father and mother (Exod. 20:12, Eph. 6:2).

The psalmist cries out, "Do not cast me off in the time of old age . . ." (Ps. 71:9).

How can we deal with the commandment and this cry?

Love is the answer. The apostle Paul affirmed that love is the greatest of virtues, surpassing even faith and hope. I know we cannot will to love; we cannot force the emotion. However, we can determine for ourselves how to live out and express our love.

"Love is patient and kind . . ." Paul wrote to the Corinthian Christians (1 Cor. 13:4). But it isn't easy to be patient with an invalid or handicapped loved one when weeks become months, and months become years.

Frustration builds and sometimes explodes into anger. Horror stories about the abuse of older people are beginning to appear more frequently.

I must confess to flashes of irritation and anger. I could not understand why Anna could not find and use the bathroom just outside her door. I got upset with Paul when he forgot, or sometimes refused, to use the grab bars I placed so strategically to help him.

My patience dissipated quickly when almost every visit to Anna included digging out dirt and excrement from under her fingernails. I became weary when I had to attach a catheter to my father-in-law every night.

And sometimes Carolyn was affected in this crossfire of frustration.

But perhaps Carolyn and I have had it easier than most couples facing this responsibility. Each of us had a parent who needed our love and care. We could lean on each other, sharing the burden and not blaming the other for the change this care imposed upon our daily lifestyle and our marriage.

17
The Magic of Love

"Love is patient and kind . . ."
1 Corinthians 13:4

It's hard to remember these characteristics and demonstrate them. When our children were growing up, it was easy to say, "Act your age!" Later I wondered which age I had in mind—child, adolescent, or young adult?

Before their deaths, my parents acted in ways that reflected their age. Good parenting has never meant forcing children to be extensions of their parents; rather, it is to model or illustrate the values and insights that will help children become responsible citizens and parents themselves. In the new parenting role we must sometimes assume for our own parents, we should also provide and model the care and security we gave our children. But our parents still must be allowed the privilege of being themselves and be given the honor and respect they deserve.

I've always considered myself a rather generous person. But I also know I am a perfectionist who feels most comfortable when schedules are kept and who prefers to solve problems rather than analyze them. It is difficult to be kind and patient if you are rigid.

It would be conveniently pious to say that the changes came as I learned to do demanding things for my parents "as unto the Lord." Intellectually, I knew we performed a service to Christ when we help those in need and in pain, but emotionally, I did not picture Christ as I combed Anna's hair or adjusted Paul's tie.

During the last years of my life with Paul and Anna, I hope that I was kind and that I became more patient. At least I became more flexible.

My "New" Parents

I came to a new perception of Paul and Anna. As children grow older, they see and understand their parents in new ways—a part of maturing. The process for me simply continued longer than I expected.

Ours was a strict, rigid family. We were Eastern European by background, polite, predictable, and not really close. We didn't embrace or kiss each other much, and we wondered about those who did.

As an only child, much was expected of me—particularly in "Christian service." After all, my father was a minister and a missionary. At the age of five I memorized Scripture (under the threat and use of a belt) and I learned a verse for each letter of the alphabet. At seven I began to play the portable pump organ at street meetings. At twelve I was pushed into a pulpit to preach.

That's a sampling of the emotional baggage I had to discard when I became a caregiver.

I could no longer see my mother as I did at age five, seven, or twelve. I had to see her as a person who was herself pushed into situations and performances for which she was not prepared and about which she had her own fears and misgivings. I had to see her as a person who was denied the affection she needed—first as an orphan and later by her husband and son.

In her later years, I tried to make up for the family's lack of affection. I realized the necessity for tactile expression of affection. I held her hand, massaged her back, and washed her face and hands—no longer with exasperation but because it was necessary. I kissed her before I left the nursing home. I'm not sure how much this meant to her, but touching was the only way we could communicate at that point.

And What about Paul?

Because my own father died when I was twenty-four (he was sixty-eight), Paul became a father to me. After all, I knew Paul for more than thirty years—longer than I knew my own father! I shared much with Paul during those three decades. I think I became the son he never had—often an argumentative, stubborn son!

But Paul was pretty rigid himself—in theology, missionary strategy, family relationships, and politics. His daughters never challenged him. I did, many times before his stroke, and often we found it possible to end such discussions in laughter rather than anger.

Things were different when he couldn't speak or respond. I didn't argue with Paul, but I became irritated and angry when I felt he needlessly endangered himself. Sometimes he tried to walk without assistance. At the nursing home he sometimes forgot or refused to use the call button for help and was found on the floor twice. At such times I exploded, then explained, and finally apologized. Paul would then wave his hand, smile his half smile, and say what sounded like, "It's all right." In those moments, I experienced Paul's forgiveness and we could begin again.

I'm sure that in caring for Paul I felt I was caring for my own father, who died too soon and whom I knew so little. I'm sure I also did some of the things I wish I could have done for Anna, my own mother. I did them not so much "as unto the Lord" as for two people whom I loved and who were my parents. In large measure, I did it for myself.

Love Must Be Real
The apostle Paul wrote to the Christians in Rome, "Let love be genuine . . ." (Rom. 12:9). Let it be sincere, not artificial. Don't try to fake it.

Paul's mind worked until his death; Anna's didn't. But I think they both sensed the authenticity of our love.

This business of parenting parents—facing and making decisions for those we love—will be easier if we remember that genuine love is patient, kind, honest, and realistic. Sometimes the expression of this love may not appear to be loving, especially when we must weigh long-term needs against short-term ones. Hard decisions have to be made for the good of our loved ones and ourselves. But we do not need to carry a burden of guilt throughout our lives if we remember and practice the criteria of love.

Let There Be Joy!

The apostle Paul wrote, "Rejoice in the Lord always . . . Let all men know your forbearance . . ." (Phil. 4:4-5). He had more than his share of woe, but he believed difficulty and depression could be overcome.

Sister Corita says, "Laughter is a sign of hope. We are saved and we can afford to laugh once in a while." Here is a practical example:

I was washing Anna's hands one day when her room- mate, Mrs. Williams, a kind and aware person, lent me a towel. In trying to keep Anna calm, I suddenly thought of an old kindergarten song and began to sing: "This is the way we wash our hands!"

Mrs. Williams picked it up, then so did Olga across the hall. Soon several of us were boisterously singing the old ditty. Anna didn't sing, but she beamed and played with the warm water. And there was laughter all around.

Anna didn't get the point of jokes any more, but she would listen to a story now and then. She liked color and pictures. She liked to watch other people, especially children, and she smiled easily and frequently.

Paul always loved to tell stories and enjoyed a good joke. We cut out cartoons and put them on his wall. He enjoyed showing "Family Circus" to his friends. It was delightful to hear his deep rumble of laughter.

A sense of humor, the gift of laughter, and an atmosphere of joy made life so much easier for Anna and Paul, and for us.

How Should We Pray?

Jesus encourages us to pray for God's will on earth, for daily bread, for deliverance from evil, and to ask in order to receive.

A great promise is found in Psalm 91:15: "When he calls to me, I will answer him; I will be with him in trouble, I will rescue him and honor him." The next verse intrigues me: "With long life I will satisfy him, and show him my salvation."

Should I pray for long life for my aging loved ones? Or should I ask the Lord to take them to be with Him? That was a hard question for Carolyn and me when we were caregivers.

Life had lost all meaning for Anna. I believed she would

be happier in heaven. Paul was still aware of life. He still had many concerns for family members, for colleagues on mission fields, and for work and ministry yet to be completed. Paul's important ministry was intercessory prayer. Should I pray that it would end—for my own convenience? No. I wanted God's will for both of them.

Since I did not know how to pray, I was grateful for Romans 8:26: "Likewise the Spirit helps us in our weakness; for we do not know how to pray as we ought, but the Spirit himself intercedes for us with sighs too deep for words."

I prayed for Carolyn and for myself, that we might be given health, patience, wisdom, and the ability to express our love to them and to ourselves.

I prayed for Anna and Paul, that God's Spirit would so surround them that they would always feel secure in His love.

And I prayed for those who cared for Anna and Paul, that they too might be given patience, wisdom, and the ability to express *their* love.

Why Bother?

Paul was often morose. Anna was detached and often did not recognize us. We certainly did not struggle to provide loving care for praise or even thanks; we got very little of this from Paul, and none from Anna.

And yet there were some good days to remember.

One day I was helping Anna with her lunch. Suddenly she smiled, reached over to touch my cheek and to feel my sport shirt. Then she took her half slice of whole wheat bread, broke it in two, and offered me a piece. For a magic moment I, too, saw the Lord in the breaking of bread. I knew we had been given a gift—the possibility and opportunity to serve two people who needed us. Somehow, through all of this, all things would work together for our good (Rom. 8:28).

Living with Hope

I read these marvelous words at Anna's graveside service:

> Who shall separate us from the love of Christ? Shall tribulation, or distress, or persecution, or famine, or nakedness, or peril, or sword? . . . No, in all these things we are more than conquerors through him who loved us. For I am sure that neither death, nor life, nor angels, nor principalities, nor things present, nor things to come, nor powers, nor height, nor depth, nor anything else in all creation (*doesn't that include the effects of stroke and senility?*), will be able to separate us from the love of God in Christ Jesus our Lord (italics mine).
> *Romans 8:35, 37-39*

Karl Barth, the great Swiss theologian, was once asked at Princeton Seminary how he would summarize his faith. His reply shocked some of the seminarians: "Jesus loves me, this I know, for the Bible tells me so!"

There's a verse of Anna Warner's old Sunday school

song that isn't often sung, but it applies beautifully to our parents who are ill or handicapped.

Jesus loves me, loves me still,
Though I'm very weak and ill;
From His shining throne on high,
Comes to watch me where I lie.

Caregivers need that reassurance, too.

Notes

Chapter One

For additional insight, listen to a recording of "Old Folks" from *Jacques Brel Is Alive and Well and Living in Paris*. Or read the play "The Gin Game" by D.L. Colburn. The language is rough, but the play deals with the loneliness and confusion of the elderly who live in an institution.

Free pamphlets on aging and coping with the elderly are available from the American Association of Retired Persons (AARP) and the Metropolitan Life Insurance Company.

Suggested reading:
Bromley, D.B. *The Psychology of Human Aging*. New York:

Penguin Books, rev. ed., 1974. Heavy reading but a classic text.

Lester, Andrew D. and Judith L. *Understanding Aging Parents*. Philadelphia: Westminster Press, 1980.

Silverstone, Barbara, and Helen Kandel Hyman. *You and Your Aging Parent*. New York: Pantheon, 1976.

Smith, Bert Kruger. *Aging in America*. Boston: Beacon Press, 1973.

Chapter Two

For information about the hospice movement, write: National Hospice Organization, 1901 N. Fort Meyer #307, Arlington, VA 22209. Or write the "original" hospice, begun by Dr. Cicely Saunders: St. Christopher's Hospice, 51/53 Lawrie Park Road, Sydenham SE26 6DZ, England.

Write Shepherd's Centers International, 5218 Oak St., Kansas City, MO 64112 to learn more about Shepherd's Centers in your area.

Suggested reading:

Maves, Paul B. *A Place to Live in Your Later Years*. Minneapolis: Augsburg Press, 1983.

Reynolds, Lillian Richter. *No Retirement: Devotions on Christian Discipleship for Older People*. Philadelphia: Fortress Press, 1984.

Chapter Three

Write the Campbell Soup Company, Box 38, Ronks, PA 17572 for information about its *Mealtime Manual*. It contains many good ideas for adapting homes for independent living, as well as recipes.

The American Red Cross offers short courses in home care.

Write Homebound Resources Ltd., P.O. Box 180082, Austin, TX 78718 for its *Caregiver's Catalog*. This is an enterprise Carolyn and I started.

The American Family Health Institute has published a series of inexpensive and practical manuals on care basics, feeding the sick, comfort measures, etc. For a listing, write Springhouse Corporation, 1111 Bethlehem Pike, Springhouse, PA 19477.

Chapter Four

Encourage the activities director or coordinator in your nursing home. He or she can always use more volunteers and other resources such as craft materials, exercise records, and "idea books." The activity director/coordinator provides a special kind of quality care, as well as awareness, to residents. This person should know about the National Association of Activity Professionals, P.O. Box 274, Park Ridge, IL 60068. A membership would be a thoughtful gift.

Suggested reading:

Manning, Doug. *When Love Gets Tough: The Nursing Home Decision*. Hereford, TX: In-Sight Books, 1983. This is an extremely helpful book. Many nursing home family councils use it as a study/discussion guide.

Chapter Five
For information about family physicians in your area, write the American Academy of Family Physicians, 1740 W. 92nd St., Kansas City, MO 64114.

Chapter Six
Check local durable medical supply houses for items that will make home care more professional and easy. Also request a home health catalog from Sears.

Bedpans, urinals, bedside commodes, elevating tables for mealtime and reading, and sturdy trapezes are readily available. Various types of incontinence pads can be purchased in supermarkets and drug stores. Discount houses often feature blood-pressure instruments and pulse-rate monitors.

Chapter Seven
Check your library or local rehabilitation center for a copy of *Paraplegia News* (or write 5201 N. 19th Ave., Phoenix, AZ 85015), published by the Paralyzed Veterans of America. It will give you many creative ideas for helping disabled persons and also sources for help.

Chapter Eight
Universities offer caregivers ongoing support and ideas through periodical newsletters. For information, write: Gerontology Center, University of Kansas, 316 Strong Hall, Lawrence, KS 66045 or Center for Study of Aging and Human Development, Duke University, Durham, NC

27710. Another source is Helpful Publications, Inc., 310 W. Durham St., Philadelphia, PA 19119-2901.

Again I stress the need for caregiver support groups. Perhaps your congregation could sponsor one. For further information, write the Child and Family Services of Michigan, Inc., P.O. Box 548, Brighton, MI 48116, and request *As Parents Grow Older.*

Chapter Nine

In your menu planning, you might want to consult such books as *Cooking with Conscience* by Alice Benjamin and Harriet Corrigan (Vineyard Books), *Diet for a Small Planet* by Frances Moore Lappe (Ballantine), or *More-With-Less Cookbook* by Doris Janzen Longacre (Herald Press). These books advocate a simple lifestyle and contain delicious and nutritious recipes.

For the visually-impaired older reader, the *Fannie Farmer Cookbook* and the *New York Times Cookbook* have been published in large-type by G.K. Hall Publishers.

Suggested reading:

Williams, Roger J. *Nutrition Against Disease*. New York: Bantam, 1973. Dr. Williams makes a strong case for the effects of poor nutrition on alcoholism and aging.

Chapter Ten

Some sources for exercise records are:

Educational Activities, Inc., P.O. Box 392, Freeport, NY 11520

Kimbo Educational Records, P.O. Box 477, Long Branch, NJ 07740

Melody House, 819 N.W. 92nd St., Oklahoma City, OK 73114

Chapter Eleven

Discover the support groups in your community. They can help you and your aging loved one.

There are many sources for cassette tapes. Begin with your state's Commission for the Blind for Library of Congress materials. Check your bookstore for recorded current bestsellers. The Jewish Guild for the Blind, Moody Bible Institute, Pacific Garden Mission ("Unshackled"), and Reigner Recording Library also provide tapes (see Resources for address list).

To stretch your loved one's mind, check with your local AARP chapter about Lifetime Learning programs. Elderhostel is another successful program, combining travel with learning.

The blue pages of your phone book often include a section on senior programs and services, including RSVP (Retired Senior Volunteer Program), ACTION, and SCORE (Service Corps of Retired Executives). You may also write The Activity Factory, 2227 Rock Island Court, Snellville, GA 30278 for its current listing.

Suggested reading:
Merrill, Toni. *Activities for the Aged and Infirm.*

Springfield, IL: Charles C. Thomas, 1977.

Peckham, Charles W. and Arline B. *Activities Keep Me Going*. Lebanon, OH: Otterbein Home, 1985.

Chapter Twelve
A do-it-yourself kit for planning your will is available from Hanley's, 22502 Orchard Lake Rd., Farmington, MI 48024.

Request a list of publications from AARP (see Resources). You may want to join.

Chapter Thirteen
Many helpful books have been written about death, dying, and grieving. One I especially like is *Don't Take My Grief Away From Me* (In-Sight Books, Hereford, TX) by Doug Manning. Check your bookstore for other current titles.

Chapter Fourteen
When visiting, get people to tell their stories. Try playing the *Ungame*—it's never threatening because no one wins.

At Homebound Resources we've created a couple items to stimulate conversation. One is *Daffy-Pull* ("How did you earn your first dollar? Tell us about it.") There are 54 memory-prompters. Another is *Re-Views,* a collection of 24 old-time picture postcards, to help people remember places and activities of an earlier time. You could even make up your own collection.

Chapter Fifteen

Suggested reading:

Becker, Arthur H. *Ministry with Older Persons*. Minneapolis: Augsburg Press, 1986.

Episcopal Society for Ministry on Aging. *Affirmative Aging: A Resource for Ministry*. Minneapolis: Winston Press, 1985.

Kerr, Horace. *How to Minister to Senior Adults in Your Church*. Nashville: Broadman Press, 1980.

Chapters Sixteen/Seventeen

As we caregivers grow older, we need to prepare ourselves for the opportunities that lie ahead. Some of the books I've found helpful are listed below.

Suggested reading:

Mace, David and Vera. *Letters to a Retired Couple*. Valley Forge: Judson Press, 1985.

Mandel, Evelyn. *The Art of Aging*. Minneapolis: Winston Press, 1981. This is a collection of challenging articles by Maggie Kuhn, Norman Cousins, Elisabeth Kübler-Ross, and others.

Smith, Tilman R. *In Favor of Growing Older*. Scottdale, PA: Herald Press, 1981.

Welliver, Dotsey. *Laughing Together: The Value of Humor in Family Life*. Elgin: Brethren Press, 1986.

Resources

Action for Independent Maturity, 1909 K. St. NW, Washington, DC 20049.

Alzheimer's Disease and Related Disorders Association, 70 E. Lake St., #600, Chicago, IL 60601-5997.

American Aging Association, University of Nebraska Medical Center, Omaha, NE 68105.

American Association of Homes for the Aging, 1050 17th St. NW, Washington, DC 20036.

American Association of Retired Persons, 1909 K Street NW, Washington, D.C. 20049.

American Bible Society, 1865 Broadway, New York, NY 10023.

American Cancer Society, 219 E. 42nd St., New York, NY 10021.

American Diabetes Association, 18 E. 48th St., New York, NY 10017.

American Foundation for the Blind, Inc., 15 W. 16th St., New York, NY 10011.

American Geriatrics Society, 10 Columbus Circle, New York, NY 10011.

American Health Care Association, 2500 15th St. NW, Washington, DC 20015.

American Heart Association, 44 W. 23rd St., New York, NY 10010.

American Lung Association, 1740 Broadway, New York, NY 10019.

American Medical Association, 535 N. Dearborn St., Chicago, IL 60610.

American Occupational Therapy Association, Inc., 6000 Executive Blvd., Rockville, MD 20852.

American Red Cross, 17th and D Sts. NW, Washington, DC 20006.

Andrus Gerontology Center, University of Southern California, Los Angeles, CA 90007. (Dr. Ethel Andrus was the founder of AARP.)

Association of Rehabilitation Facilities, 5530 Wisconsin Ave. NW, Washington, DC 20015.

Center for the Study of Aging and Human Development, Duke University, Durham, NC 27710.

Concern for Dying (an educational council), 250 W. 57th St., New York, NY 10107.

Continental Association of Funeral and Memorial Societies, 1828 L St. NW, Washington, DC 20036.

Elderhostel, 80 Boyleston St., #400, Boston, MA 02116.

Episcopal Society for Ministry on Aging, Inc., Sayre Hall, 317 Wyandotte St., Bethlehem, PA 18015.

Family Service Association of America, 44 W. 23rd St., New York, NY 10010.

Gerontological Society, 1 Dupont Circle, Washington, DC 20036.

Gray Panthers, 3635 Chestnut St., Philadelphia, PA 19104.

Homebound Resources, Ltd., P.O. Box 180082, Austin, TX 78718.

Homemakers' Home and Health Care Services, 3651 Van Rick Drive, Kalamazoo, MI 49001.

Jewish Guild for the Blind, 15 W. 65th St., New York, NY 10023.

Living Bank, P.O. Box 6725, Houston, TX 77005.

Lutheran Braille Workers, Inc., Sight-Saving Division, 495 9th Ave., San Francisco, CA 94118.

Moody Bible Institute, 820 N. LaSalle Dr., Chicago, IL 60610.

National Association for Mental Health, 1800 North Kent St., Arlington, VA 22209.

National Association for Visually Handicapped, 305 E. 24th St., New York, NY 10010.

National Association of the Deaf, 814 Thayer Ave., Silver Spring, MD 20910.

National Association of Hearing and Speech Agencies, 814 Thayer Ave., Silver Spring, MD 20910.

National Caucus on the Black Aged, 1730 M St. NW, Washington, DC 20036.

National Council on the Aging, 600 Maryland Ave. SW, West Wing 100, Washington, DC 20024.

National Council for Homemaker-Home Health Aide Services, 67 Irving Place, New York, NY 10003.

National Council of Senior Citizens, 1511 K St. NW, Room 202, Washington, DC 20005.

National Interfaith Coalition on Aging, Inc., P.O. Box 1924, Athens, GA 30603.

National Retired Teachers Association, 1901 K St. NW, Washington DC 20036.

New Eyes for the Needy, Inc., Short Hills, NJ 07078.

Dr. Garland O'Quinn, Jr., Physical Activity Consultant, P.O. Box 4548, Austin, TX 78765.

Pacific Garden Mission, 646 S. State St., Chicago, IL 60605.

Preventicare, Lawrence Frankel Foundation, Virginia and Brooks St., Charleston, WV 25301.

Reigner Recording Library, Union Theological Seminary, Richmond, VA 23227.

U.S. Administration on Aging, 3303 C St. SW, HHS South, Washington, DC 20024. (Administers ten regional offices. Each state has its own Department, Office, or Commission on Aging, usually located in the state capital.)

Index